THREE SISTERS

Anton Chekhov

*New English Version
by Richard Nelson*

*Based on a literal
translation from the
Russian by
Olga Lifson*

357 W 20th St., NY NY 10011
212 627-1055

THREE SISTERS
© Copyright 1991 Richard Nelson

First printing: December 1991
ISBN: 0-88145-098-7

Book design: Marie Donovan
Word processing: WordMarc Composer Plus
Typographic controls: Xerox Ventura Publisher 2.0 PE
Typeface: Palatino
Printed on recycled acid-free paper, and bound in the USA.

BY RICHARD NELSON
PUBLISHED BY
BROADWAY PLAY PUBLISHING INC

Plays

AN AMERICAN COMEDY (Mark Taper Forum)
BAL (In the anthology ANTI-NATURALISM;
  Goodman Theater)
BETWEEN EAST AND WEST (Hampstead Theatre
  Club, Yale Rep)
JUNGLE COUP (In the anthology PLAYS FROM
  PLAYWRIGHTS HORIZONS)
RIP VAN WINKLE OR "THE WORKS" (Yale Rep)
ROOTS IN WATER (River Arts Rep, BBC 3)

Adaptations

DON JUAN by Molière (Arena Stage)
IL CAMPIELLO by Carlo Goldoni (The Acting
  Company)
THE MARRIAGE OF FIGARO by Beaumarchais
  (Guthrie Theater and Broadway)

ABOUT THE AUTHOR

Richard Nelson's other plays include TWO
SHAKESPEAREAN ACTORS (Royal Shakespeare
Company), SENSIBILITY AND SENSE (American
Playhouse Television), THE END OF A SENTENCE
(American Playhouse), PRINCIPIA SCRIPTORIAE
(Manhattan Theater Club and the Royal Shakespeare
Company), THE RETURN OF PINOCCHIO, THE
VIENNA NOTES, CONJURING AN EVENT, and
THE KILLING OF YABLONSKI.

His other translations and adaptations include
Brecht's JUNGLE OF CITIES and THE WEDDING
(BAM Theater Company), Erdman's THE SUICIDE
(Arena Stage and The Goodman Theater), and Fo's
ACCIDENTAL DEATH OF AN ANARCHIST
(Broadway). He also is the author of the book for the
Broadway musical CHESS, and numerous radio plays
for the BBC.

Nelson has received a London TIME OUT Theatre
Award, two Giles Cooper Awards, two Obies, a
Guggenheim Fellowship, two Rockefeller Playwriting
Grants, two National Endowment for the Arts
Playwriting Fellowships, and a Lila Wallace *Reader's
Digest* Fund Writer's Award.

ORIGINAL PRODUCTION

This version of THREE SISTERS was first produced
by the Guthrie Theater (Liviu Ciulei, Artistic Director)
on 28 June 1984 with the following cast and creative
contributors:

OLGA .... Trish Hawkins
IRINA .... Frances McDormand
CHEBUTYKIN .... Michael Egan
TUZENBACH .... Paul Walker
MASHA .... Joan MacIntosh
SOLYONY .... Randle Mell
ANFISA .... June Gibbons
FERAPONT .... Roger DeKoven
VERSHININ .... Gerry Bamman
ANDREI .... Jay Patterson
KULYGIN .... John M Towey
NATASHA .... Mary McDonnell
FEDOTIK .... Richard Howard
RODE .... David Rasmussen
Officers, soldiers, mummers, & maids ....
Thomas Robert Burke, Jay Disney
Therese V Sherman, Hayden Saunier
James Naiden

Director and scenic designer .... Liviu Ciulei
Costume designer .... Jack Edwards
Lighting designer .... Dawn Chiang
Dramaturg .... Michael Lupu

CHARACTERS

ANDREI SERGEYEVICH PROZOROV
NATALYA (NATASHA) *his fiancée, later his wife*
OLGA
MASHA
IRINA, *his three sisters*
FYODOR ILYICH KULYGIN, *a high school teacher,*
  MASHA's *husband*
ALEXANDER IGNATYEVICH VERSHININ, *a lieutenant
  colonel, battery commander*
BARON NIKOLAI LVOVICH TUZENBACH, *a lieutenant*
VASSILY VASSILYCH SOLYONY, *a captain*
IVAN ROMANICH CHEBUTYKIN, *a military doctor*
ALEXEI PETROVICH FEDOTIK, *a second lieutenant*
VLADIMIR KARLOVICH RODE, *a second lieutenant*
FERAPONT, *an old porter from the District Council*
ANFISA, *the* PROZOROVS' *old nanny*
Officers, soldiers, mummers, and maids

The action of the play takes place in and around the
PROZOROVS' house, in a provincial town of Russia at
the turn of the century. It covers a period of four years.

ACT ONE: Springtime. Midday.
ACT TWO: A year and a half later. January. Evening.
ACT THREE: Two years after ACT TWO. Three
  o'clock in the morning.
ACT FOUR: The same year. Autumn. Mid-day.

ACT ONE

(Prozorovs' house. The living room; behind is seen the ballroom. Mid-day; outside the sun shines brightly. In the ballroom a table is being set for lunch.)

(OLGA wears the standard dress of a girl's high-school teacher. She walks as she corrects exercise books. MASHA wears black; her hat is on her lap; she sits and reads a book. IRINA is in white; she stands to one side, deep in thought.)

OLGA: One year ago on this very day, May fifth—on your birthday, Irina—Father died. It was bitter cold and snowing. At the time, it all seemed more than I could bear; you fainted, I even thought you'd died. Now, a year's gone by, we think about it quite easily. You're back wearing white; your face glows. *(Clock strikes twelve.)* The clock struck then, too. *(Pause)* I remember them carrying Father away. The band played a march, they fired rifle shots over the grave. For a general of the brigade there weren't many mourners. Well, it was raining hard, rain mixed with snow.

IRINA: Why think about it?

(BARON TUZENBACH, CHEBUTYKIN, and SOLYONY appear by the table in the ballroom.)

OLGA: Now today it's warm. We can even keep the windows open. Though there still aren't any leaves on the birches. It's been eleven years since Father was put in charge of the brigade and we all had to leave

Moscow. I remember well that at this time, in early
May, in Moscow all the trees already have leaves, it is
warm, the sun bathes everything. After eleven years,
I remember it all as if it were yesterday. Oh God,
when I woke up this morning and saw the sunshine,
that golden light, and smelled the spring coming,
it made me so happy, I longed to go home.

CHEBUTYKIN: Like hell!

TUZENBACH: It's nonsense, of course.

(MASHA, *lost in her book, whistles softly.*)

OLGA: Masha, don't whistle. How can you? It's not
polite. *(Pause)* Every morning school, every afternoon
and night tutoring. It's no wonder I get those
headaches. I've started to think like an old woman.
Really, after four years of this work, it feels as if day
after day all my strength, my youth, is being drained
out of me, squeezed, drop by drop. All that's alive
inside me now and grows is that longing....

IRINA: To go to Moscow! Sell the house, leave
everything, and to Moscow!

(CHEBUTYKIN *and* TUZENBACH *laugh.*)

OLGA: Yes, to Moscow, just as soon as we can.

IRINA: Brother's bound to be a professor soon, so he
won't be staying here. But then there is poor Masha.

OLGA: Masha will spend every summer with us in
Moscow.

(MASHA *whistles softly.*)

IRINA: God willing, it will all work out. *(Looks out the
window)* It's wonderful out today. I'm not sure why
but I feel so happy. This morning I remembered that it
was my birthday...I suddenly felt so happy. I thought
about when we were children, when Mother was still
alive. The thoughts I had, such thoughts.

OLGA: How radiant you look today; I've never seen you more lovely. Masha is beautiful too. Andrei could be quite handsome, but he's put on weight, it doesn't become him. But me—I've grown older and skinnier. I suppose it's the girls at school who are wearing me down. Today I'm free. I'm home. I don't have a headache, and I feel younger than I did yesterday. I am only twenty-eight.... God's in His heaven, all's right with the world. Though sometimes I think if I'd gotten married and been able to stay home, it would have been even better. *(Pause)* I would love my husband.

TUZENBACH: *(To* SOLYONY*)* I'm tired of listening to this drivel. *(Entering into the living room)* I forgot to tell you that Vershinin, the new lieutenant-colonel of the brigade, will be paying you a visit today.

OLGA: How nice.

IRINA: Is he old?

TUZENBACH: *(Plays softly)* Not really. Forty, forty-five at the most. He seems nice enough. He certainly has a head on his shoulders; only he talks a little too much.

IRINA: An interesting man?

TUZENBACH: I suppose so.... But there's a wife, a mother-in-law, and two daughters. It's his second marriage. He pays visits and tells everyone he has a wife and two daughters. He'll tell you too when he's here. His wife's pretty odd; she wears her hair in a long braid, like little girls do; she seems rather pompous— she's always talking philosophy; also, she keeps trying to kill herself, apparently to annoy her husband. If I were in his place, I'd have left her a long time ago, but he bears it, and just complains to everyone.

SOLYONY: *(Entering with* CHEBUTYKIN *from the ballroom)* With one hand I lift fifty-four pounds. With two—180, maybe 200. Conclusion: Two men are not twice as strong as one, but three times, even more.

CHEBUTYKIN: *(Reading a newspaper as he walks)* Cure for baldness: take an ounce of naphthalene, one half bottle of alcohol, mix and apply daily. Let's make a note of that. *(Does. To* SOLYONY:*)* As I was saying, tightly cork the bottle, push the glass tube through the cork...then withdraw a small amount of ordinary alum....

IRINA: Ivan Romanich, dear Ivan Romanich!

CHEBUTYKIN: What is it, my princess?

IRINA: Tell me why I'm so happy today. I keep seeing myself floating under a huge blue sky with great white birds around me. Why is that?

CHEBUTYKIN: *(Kisses her hands, tenderly)* You are *my* great white bird....

IRINA: This morning I woke up, got out of bed, washed myself, and suddenly everything became clear to me, I understand the meaning of life. Dear Ivan Romanich, I understand everything. Everyone must work, work by the sweat of his brow, whoever he is. This is our true goal in life, our happiness, our ambition. How wonderful it must be to be a laborer who gets up at the crack of dawn to break rocks in the street, or a shepherd, or a schoolteacher helping the children to learn, or a worker on the railroad.... My God, if I can't be a man who works, then I'd rather be an ox or plow horse or any other working animal, than a young woman who gets up at noon, has breakfast in bed, and takes two hours getting dressed.... It's horrible! The way a man craves water on a hot day, that's how I crave work. And if in the future I'm not getting up early and going to work, dear Ivan Romanich, I want you never to speak to me again.

CHEBUTYKIN: *(Tenderly)* I won't. I won't.

OLGA: Father taught us all to get up by seven. Irina still wakes up then, but stays in bed at least till nine, thinking about who knows what—and with such a serious look on her face. *(Laughs)*

IRINA: You keep forgetting that I am no longer a little girl. I am twenty years old!

TUZENBACH: The longing for work. God, I can understand that! I've never worked in my life. St. Petersburg, where I was born, is itself a cold and lazy city. My family never even knew what work was, we never had to worry. I remember that when I'd come home from cadet school, I'd make it hard for the footman to take off my boots, just for the fun of it, and Mother would just watch and smile. For her, I could do no wrong. They shielded me from work; they almost succeeded, almost! But times are changing. A powerful cleansing storm has gathered; it is coming nearer and nearer; soon it will sweep our world of its laziness, its indifference, its prejudice against work, and its god-forsaken boredom. I will work, and within twenty-five, thirty years, we will all be working! Every one of us.

CHEBUTYKIN: Not me.

TUZENBACH: You don't count.

SOLYONY: In twenty-five years you'll be dead. Thank God. In two, three, you'll have had your stroke; if not I'll have put a bullet in your skull out of impatience. *(Takes a perfume bottle out of his pocket and sprinkles it on his chest and hands)*

CHEBUTYKIN: *(Laughs)* And I've never done anything in my life. After university, I never again lifted a

finger, never even opened a book, just newspapers....
(*Takes a newspaper*) Here, I know from the paper that
there's a writer named Dobrolyubov. But what did he
write? I don't know.... God only knows.... (*Pounding is
heard on the floor*) They're knocking downstairs. That
must be for me. A visitor. I'll be back.... Wait here...
(*Hurries out, combing his beard*)

IRINA: He's up to something.

TUZENBACH: Yes. He had a peculiar look on his face
when he went out. My guess is he's gone to get you
your present.

IRINA: Oh, I wish he wouldn't!

OLGA: He does do the silliest things.

MASHA: "A green oak stands by the sea.
A golden chain around it...
A golden chain around it...."
(*She stands, hums softly.*)

OLGA: You're not happy today, Masha.

(MASHA *hums, putting on her hat.*)

OLGA: Are you going somewhere?

MASHA: Home.

IRINA: That's strange....

TUZENBACH: But what about the party?

MASHA: What about it? I'll be back this evening.
Good-bye, dear. (*Kisses* IRINA) Once again—happy
birthday! When Father was alive there'd be thirty,
forty officers at our birthdays—the house was full of
noise. Today there's one man and a half, and it's as
quiet as death. I'm going.... I'm in a strange mood
today, just ignore me. (*Laughs through her tears*)
We'll talk later. I'll go somewhere.

IRINA: (*Displeased*) Really, how can you....

OLGA: *(Crying)* I understand, Masha.

SOLYONY: Let a man try to talk philosophy, and it'll come out as philosophy or—at least—sophistry. But when a woman talks philosophy, it comes out sounding like knuckles being cracked.

MASHA: What is that supposed to mean? You awful man....

SOLYONY: "Before the peasant could even gasp for air, His chest was crushed in the arms of the bear." *(Pause)*

MASHA: *(Angrily to* OLGA*)* Stop that whimpering!

(Enter ANFISA *and* FERAPONT *with a cake)*

ANFISA: Come on. Come on. Your feet are clean. I checked. *(To* IRINA*)* From the District Council office, compliments of Chairman Protopopov.... It's a cake.

IRINA: Thank you. Please thank him. *(She takes the cake.)*

FERAPONT: What?

IRINA: *(Louder)* Please thank him!

OLGA: Give him a piece of pie, Anfisa. Ferapont, go get your piece of pie.

FERAPONT: What?

ANFISA: A piece of pie, she said. Come on. Come on. What's wrong with you, can't you hear? And pick up your feet. *(They exit.)*

MASHA: I don't like this Protopopov. He shouldn't be invited here.

IRINA: I haven't invited him.

MASHA: Good.

(Enter CHEBUTYKIN, *followed by a* SOLDIER *carrying a silver samovar. There are exclamations of astonishment and dissatisfaction.)*

OLGA: *(Covering her face with her hands)* A samovar! How could you! How could he! *(She exits into the ballroom, goes to the table.)*

*(*IRINA, MASHA, *and* TUZENBACH *talk at the same time. Their lines overlap.)*

IRINA: My dear Doctor, what could you have been thinking?

MASHA: Ivan Romanich!...

TUZENBACH: *(Laughing)* What did I tell you?

IRINA: Everyone knows samovars should only be given to one's wife!

MASHA: He's shameless!

CHEBUTYKIN: My dear ones, you...you three are all I have in the world, you're everything I care about. I'm past sixty, I'm a lonely, useless, tired old man. The only thing good about me is my love for you. Without that I'd have died long ago.... *(To* IRINA*)* My Princess, I've known you all my life. I cradled you in my arms.... I loved your dear mother....

MASHA: But Irina is not your wife!

IRINA: Such an expensive present.

CHEBUTYKIN: *(Mimicking* IRINA*)* Such an expensive present.... What are you talking about. *(To the* SOLDIER*)* Put it there! *(Mimicking)* Such an expensive present....

ANFISA: *(Entering)* A gentleman is here. I don't know him. He's taking off his coat. He's coming up. Now Irina, you behave yourself, mind your manners. He's a colonel. *(Goes into the ballroom)* The lunch is ready and no one's at the table! *(Exits)*

TUZENBACH: Must be Vershinin.

(Enter VERSHININ)

TUZENBACH: Lieutenant-Colonel Vershinin!

VERSHININ: *(To MASHA and IRINA)* Allow me this pleasure of introducing myself: My name is Vershinin. I have been looking forward to finally meeting you. So you're all grown up. My...my...

IRINA: Please sit down. We are very pleased that you came.

VERSHININ: *(Happily)* On the contrary, it is I who am pleased. I can't tell you how pleased. But weren't there three sisters? Three girls...I wouldn't remember the faces, but your father, I am positive, had three little girls. I saw them with my own eyes. But that was long ago. How time flies.

TUZENBACH: Colonel Vershinin comes from Moscow.

IRINA: From Moscow? You're from Moscow?

VERSHININ: Yes, Moscow. Your father commanded a battery there, I was an officer in the same brigade. *(To MASHA)* Your face seems familiar.

MASHA: I don't remember yours.

IRINA: Olga! Olga! Come here, Olga.

(OLGA comes out of the ballroom.)

IRINA: It seems Lieutenant-Colonel Vershinin comes from Moscow.

VERSHININ: You are obviously Olga Sergheevna, the eldest, and you, then, Masha, and you the youngest, Irina....

OLGA: You're really from Moscow?

VERSHININ: I am. I went to the cadet school in Moscow and stayed to join the army. I served there for years, until finally given my own battery, and, as you can see, transferred here. I really don't recognize you, I only remember there being three sisters. Your father I remember vividly. I just have to close my eyes and I can see him as if he were still alive. I used to visit your house in Moscow.

OLGA: I thought I remembered everyone and now....

VERSHININ: My name is Alexander Ignatevich Vershinin.

IRINA: Alexander Ignatevich—from Moscow! This *is* exciting!

OLGA: You see, we're moving back there.

IRINA: We should be there by fall. It's our home town, we were all born there, on Old Basmanny Street....

(They both laugh with delight.)

MASHA: What do you know, someone from home! *(Suddenly)* I remember now: Olga, remember that officer they called "the love-sick major"? You were only a lieutenant then, and you were in love with somebody, but for some reason they all teased you and called you "major".

VERSHININ: *(Laughs)* That's me...the love-sick major! Right.

MASHA: You had just a moustache then. You seem so much older. *(Through her tears)* So much older!

VERSHININ: Yes, when I was called the love-sick major, I was still young and still in love. Now, no more...

OLGA: Still your hair isn't gray yet; you're *older*, maybe, but not *old*.

VERSHININ: I'm forty-two. Have you been away from Moscow long?

IRINA: Eleven years. Masha, don't be silly, what are you crying about? *(Crying)* Now I'm crying.

MASHA: It's nothing. Nothing. And where did you live?

VERSHININ: On Old Basmanny Street.

OLGA: So did we.

VERSHININ: For a while I lived on Niemetskaya Street.... I could walk to the barracks. But there was that dark little bridge in between. Just to cross it, with the black water rushing down below, was enough to make a lonely man deeply depressed. *(Pause)* But here you have a real river! A wide, beautiful river!

OLGA: Yes, but it gets so cold here. In the winter, it's the cold, and in the summer, it's the mosquitoes.

VERSHININ: What do you mean?! You have here a fine, healthy Russian climate. You have a forest, the river...and the birches. Those dear modest birches; they're my favorite trees. It's a good place to live. Except that the railroad station happens to be fifteen miles out of town.... And no one knows why that is.

SOLYONY: I know why.

(All look at him.)

SOLYONY: If it were near it wouldn't be far, and because it is far, it can't be near.

(Awkward pause)

TUZENBACH: Vassily Vassilych—is always joking.

OLGA: Now I know who you are. I remember.

VERSHININ: I also knew your mother.

CHEBUTYKIN: A good woman, God rest her soul.

IRINA: Mother's buried in Moscow.

OLGA: In the Novo-Devitchy Cemetery.

MASHA: Do you believe that I'm beginning to forget her face?!... What she looked like. We'll all be forgotten one day—just forgotten.

VERSHININ: Yes, forgotten! That is our fate, there's no escape. As time goes by, everything we now think is important, significant, and momentous in our lives will be forgotten or considered trivial. *(Pause)* It's interesting: We have no way of knowing how the future will see our world, what it will deem important, what worthwhile, and what ludicrous. After all, weren't the discoveries of, say, Copernicus and Columbus ridiculed in their time, while the scribblings of some fool praised as immortal truth? So who can say that the way we live today—this comfortable and civilized life—will not one day be looked upon as strange, confused, barbaric, even unhealthy, perhaps even evil....

TUZENBACH: Who knows? But who can say our age won't be seen as noble and progressive? We have abolished torture and capital punishment, we're not at war—yet there is still so much suffering.

SOLYONY: Cluck-cluck-cluck. Instead of pecking at corn, he pecks at philosophy.

TUZENBACH: Vassily Vassilych, please leave me alone. *(Moves to another place)* I'm beginning to get a little tired of you.

SOLYONY: Cluck-cluck-cluck.

TUZENBACH: *(To* VERSHININ*)* The very fact that we now notice the suffering in our world—and much suffering there is—only goes to show how much we have improved morally.

VERSHININ: Yes, yes, of course.

CHEBUTYKIN: You've suggested, Baron, that our age may one day be seen as a great one; but still, people are very small. *(Stands up)* Look how small I am. You're only saying my life is noble to make me feel better. And why not?

(Violin is heard off.)

MASHA: That's Andrei our brother playing.

IRINA: He's our scholar. He's going to be a professor. Father was a soldier, but his son will be a professor.

MASHA: Father wanted that.

OLGA: We've been teasing him all day. We think he's a little taken with a girl.

IRINA: She's from the town. She'll probably be by today.

MASHA: The way she dresses! It's not enough to say she's unfashionable, she's downright pitiful. Imagine wearing a bright yellow skirt with some vulgar trim together with a red blouse. And her cheeks, rubbed almost raw. I can't believe it's anything serious; Andrei still has taste. He's just trying to tease us. Yesterday I heard she was going to marry Protopopov, the chairman of the district council. That's just as well. *(Goes to the side door)* Andrei, come out for a minute. Please come out, dear!

(ANDREI enters.)

OLGA: My brother, Andrei.

VERSHININ: My name is Vershinin.

ANDREI: Mine is Prozorov *(Wipes sweat from his face)* You've come to take command of the battery?

OLGA: Alexander Ignatevich is from Moscow!

ANDREI: My sympathies. My sisters will never leave you alone now.

VERSHININ: It is I, I believe, who have already bored them.

IRINA: See this frame? Andrei gave it to me today. *(Shows it)* He made it himself.

VERSHININ: *(Looks at the frame; doesn't know what to say)* Yes...it's quite...quite....

IRINA: He made that frame on the piano, too.

(ANDREI, annoyed, waves his hand and walks away.)

OLGA: He has his degree, plays the violin, carves all sorts of things out of wood, he's a man of many talents. Don't walk away, Andrei! He's always walking away. Come back here!

(MASHA and IRINA take his arms and laughingly lead him back.)

MASHA: Come on. Come on.

ANDREI: Please, just leave me alone.

MASHA: Don't be silly. Alexander Ignatevich used to be called the love-sick major. And he didn't mind.

VERSHININ: Not at all.

MASHA: Maybe I should call you the love-sick fiddler!

IRINA: Or the love-sick professor!

OLGA: He's in love! Our little Andrei's in love!

IRINA: *(Applauds)* Bravo! Andrei's in love! Andrei's in love! Andrei's in love!

CHEBUTYKIN: *(Goes up behind ANDREI and puts his arms around him)* Man was created by God to love,
And not just Him who is above!
(Roars with laughter; holding his newspaper)

ANDREI: That's enough! Quite enough, thank you.
(Wipes his face) I didn't sleep at all last night. I'm not
completely myself today. I read till four, then tried
lying down, but I kept thinking about one thing or
another. Then I watched the sun creep into my room
and across my bed. This summer, while I'm still here,
I think I'll translate a book from English.

VERSHININ: You read English?

ANDREI: Yes. Father, may he rest in peace, educated
us with a vengeance. This may sound foolish, but it's
true—since his death, I've gained I don't know how
many pounds, it's like my body's suddenly been
freed and can do what it wants. Thanks to Father, my
sisters and I know French, German, as well as English.
Irina even Italian. But we all paid a price.

MASHA: Three languages is an unnecessary luxury
in a town like this; in fact, it's not even a luxury, it's
simply superfluous, like a sixth finger. We know too
much.

VERSHININ: Amazing! *(Laughs)* So you know too
much! I'm sorry, but I don't believe that in even the
most empty and backward town there isn't a need for
the educated person. Let's take this town; out of what,
a hundred thousand people, let's say there are only
three like yourselves. Obviously, you won't be able
to defeat the ignorance of the crowd which surrounds
you. During your lifetime you will be forced to give
in. And in time you will lose yourselves in the masses
of this hundred thousand. Life will suffocate you. Yet
you won't completely disappear; your influence will
be lasting. And in time, others like you will appear,
first six, then twelve, until you are now the many.
In two or three hundred years, life on this great
earth will be unspeakably beautiful and miraculous.
Mankind needs such a life; and even though we
have not found it yet, we must envision it, wait for it,

dream of it, and prepare for it. And for this to be, it is our duty to see and know more than did our parents and our parents' parents. *(Laughs)* And you complain that you know too much!

MASHA: *(Taking off her hat)* I'm staying for lunch.

IRINA: *(Sighs)* Yes! We should have written that down.

(ANDREI has gone out, unnoticed.)

TUZENBACH: You say that in some future time, life on this earth will be glorious. I couldn't agree more. But if we wish to take part in this life now, even if in a small way, we must get ourselves ready, we must work....

VERSHININ: *(Getting up)* Yes. My, my, so many flowers. *(Looks around)* And such a beautiful home! I envy you! For me it's always been rented rooms; just a couple of chairs, a sofa, and always a stove that smokes. For my whole life I've missed having flowers like these.... *(Rubs his hands)* But what can you do?

TUZENBACH: Yes, we must work. You're probably thinking—how typically German to be so idealistic. But don't let the name Tuzenbach fool you—I am thoroughly Russian. I don't even know German. My father belonged to the Orthodox Church....

VERSHININ: *(Walking around)* I've often wondered: What if I could begin my life again, knowing everything I know now. What if a man's life could be only a rough draft from which to make a more clean, finished copy, so to speak. I think we'd all like to have done things differently; another life, where the rooms have flowers and sunlight.... I have a wife and two daughters. My wife is not a healthy person, et cetera, et cetera. If I could begin again I wouldn't get married.... No, no!

(KULYGIN enters in his schoolteacher's uniform.)

KULYGIN: *(Going up to* IRINA*)* My dear sister-in-law, let me wish you a happy birthday from the bottom of my heart, may you have health and all the happiness in the world. Allow me to present you with this gift. *(Gives it to her)* It's a book. A history of our high school over the last fifty years. Written by me. An unimportant little book, I wrote it because I had nothing better to do. But read it anyway. Good afternoon gentlemen. *(To* VERSHININ*)* My name is Kulygin. Teacher at the high school. Also the third assistant dean. *(To* IRINA*)* You'll find in it a list of all the graduates for the last fifty years. *Feci quod potui, faciant melior potentes.* *(Kisses* MASHA*)*

IRINA: You gave me a copy for Easter.

KULYGIN: *(Laughs)* I didn't! I did? Then...I shall take it back. On second thought, let's give it to the colonel. We read all sorts of things if we're bored enough.

VERSHININ: Thank you. *(Prepares to go)* It was a pleasure to have finally met you....

OLGA: You're not going so soon. No, no.

IRINA: You have to stay for lunch. Please.

OLGA: Yes, please do!

VERSHININ: *(Bows)* I seem to have barged in on your birthday. Forgive me, I didn't know, and I haven't offered my own best wishes....

(He goes with OLGA *into the ballroom.)*

KULYGIN: Gentlemen, today is Sunday, the day of rest, so—let's rest and enjoy ourselves, each according to his age and rank. These rugs should be stored over the summer; keep them for winter. I suggest mothballs.... The Romans knew how to live, they knew when to work and when to relax. *Mens sana in corpore sano.* They had a time and place for everything. Our principal says: "The most important things in life are form and structure. What loses its form ceases to exist." That holds true even for our daily lives. *(Takes* MASHA *by the waist, laughing)* Masha loves me. My wife loves me. Those curtains should be stored as well.... I'm quite happy with life today. Masha, we're due at the principal's at four. There's to be a little outing for all the teachers and their families.

MASHA: I'm not going.

KULYGIN: *(Hurt)* But why not, Masha?

MASHA: Let's talk about it later.... *(Angrily)* All right, I'll go, now please, stop pestering me.... *(Moves to one side)*

KULYGIN: Then we're to spend the evening at the principal's. Despite his health, he still insists on being sociable. A splendid, exemplary man. He said to me yesterday after the committee meeting, he said to me: "I'm tired, Fyodor Ilych, I'm tired." *(Looks at the clock, then his watch)* Your clock is seven minutes fast. "Yes," he said, "I'm tired."

(Violin is heard.)

(OLGA returns. Gradually, they all go to the table in the back as they speak.)

OLGA: Please, everyone, come to the table! Wait until you see the meat pie!

KULYGIN: Dear, dear Olga. I worked yesterday from early morning to eleven at night. I was exhausted. Today I'm relaxing. *(Goes into the ballroom)*

CHEBUTYKIN: *(Puts his paper down; combs his beard)* Did someone mention a pie?

MASHA: *(Severely, to* CHEBUTYKIN*)* Just remember: You're not to have anything to drink today. Do you hear me? It's not good for you.

CHEBUTYKIN: What?! I haven't been drunk for two years. *(Impatiently)* Besides, sober/drunk, it's all the same.

MASHA: Still... Now don't you dare! *(Angrily, under her breath so her husband doesn't hear)* One more insufferable evening at the principal's. Hell!

TUZENBACH: I wouldn't go, if I were you.... It's that simple.

CHEBUTYKIN: Yes, don't go.

MASHA: Right. Don't go.... You can't call this a life.... Damn it! *(Goes into the ballroom)*

CHEBUTYKIN: *(Following her)* Now, now, now...

SOLYONY: *(Going into the ballroom)* Cluck-cluck-cluck...

TUZENBACH: Really, Vassily Vasilevich, that is quite enough! You've made your point.

SOLYONY: Cluck-cluck-cluck...

KULYGIN: *(Happily)* To your health, Colonel! I'm an educator myself and I am quite at home here. I'm Masha's husband.... She's a good soul. A very good soul.

VERSHININ: I'll try some of this dark vodka.... *(Drinks, to OLGA)* I feel so incredibly comfortable here!

(They are all at the table in the back. IRINA and TUZENBACH are left alone in the living room.)

IRINA: Masha's not herself today. She was eighteen when they got married. Then she thought he was the brightest man in the world. It's different now. He's one of the kindest, just not one of the brightest.

OLGA: *(Impatiently)* Andrei, are you joining us or not?

ANDREI: *(Off)* I'm coming! *(Enters and goes to the table)*

TUZENBACH: What are you thinking about?

IRINA: I don't like this friend of yours, Solyony; he scares me. He says the stupidest things.

TUZENBACH: He is a strange man. I feel sorry for him really, though he can get under your skin. I think he's shy. When it's just the two of us, he's fine, even gentle. But in a group, he becomes obnoxious and crude. Don't go, they won't miss us yet. Stay near me. What are you thinking about? *(Pause)* You're twenty. I'm not even thirty. Think of all the years we have ahead of us, the days followed by days, each waiting to be filled with my love for you....

IRINA: Nikolai Lvovich, don't talk about love.

TUZENBACH: *(Not hearing her)* I hunger to live, to struggle, to work, and this hunger is now inseparable from my love for you, Irina, you are so beautiful, you even make life seem beautiful.What are you thinking about?

IRINA: You say, "Life is beautiful!" And what if it only seems that way? So far, life has not been beautiful for us, three sisters; it's only been stifling us...like weeds trying to choke us.... I'm crying. I shouldn't.... No... No... *(Dries her eyes, smiles)* We must work, work... that's why we're not happy and life seems sad. We don't know what work is. Our sort of people have disdained work.

(NATASHA IVANOVNA *enters. She is wearing a pink dress and a green sash.)*

NATASHA: They're already at lunch.... I'm late.... *(Hurriedly looks at herself in the mirror and straightens her clothes)* My hair looks fine.... *(Sees* IRINA*)* Dear Irina Sergheevna, happy birthday! *(Kisses her tenderly and at length)* There's so many people! I won't have anything to say.... Baron, how do you do?

OLGA: *(Entering from the ballroom)* Natasha's here.
How are you? *(Kisses her)*

NATASHA: The same to you. You have so many
guests.... I am so shy.

OLGA: Come along, they're all just friends. *(Under her
breath, shocked, to* NATASHA*)* A green sash, dear? What
could you have been thinking of?

NATASHA: What's wrong with wearing green? *(Does it
bring bad luck?)*

OLGA: It's just that it doesn't go.... It does look strange.

NATASHA: *(Almost in tears)* It does? It's not too green,
only a little green.

(Goes into the ballroom with OLGA*. They all have sat
down; the living room is empty.)*

KULYGIN: May this year find you a husband, Irina.
It's getting to be that time.

CHEBUTYKIN: Natasha, I wish you the same.

KULYGIN: But Natasha is already very close to getting
one.

MASHA: *(Raps her plate with a fork)* I'll have a drink too.
You only live once!

KULYGIN: No good conduct stars for you today,
Masha.

VERSHININ: This home-made vodka is rather good.
What's it made from?

SOLYONY: Cockroaches.

IRINA: Yuck! That's disgusting!

OLGA: For dinner tonight it's turkey and sweet apple
pie. I can't tell you how nice it is to spend a whole day
at home. You'll all be back for dinner, I hope.

VERSHININ: May I come as well?

IRINA: Please.

NATASHA: In this house you never have to ask.

CHEBUTYKIN: "Man was created by God to love,
And not just Him who is above!" *(Laughs)*

ANDREI: *(Angry)* Please don't. Aren't you getting tired
of that?

(FEDOTIK and RODE enter with a large basket of flowers.)

FEDOTIK: It looks like they're already eating.

RODE: Eating? Yes, they're eating....

FEDOTIK: Hold it! *(Takes a photograph)* That's one. Hold
it again. *(Takes another)* That's two. Now we're ready!

*(They take the basket into the ballroom, where they are
received with great noise.)*

RODE: *(Loudly)* Happy birthday and many happy
returns! Nice day out today. I've been out with the
high-school students. You know I teach them
gymnastics.

FEDOTIK: *(Takes another photograph)* It's all right if you
move, Irina Sergheevna. You're looking exceptionally
well today. *(Takes a top out of his pocket)* Here, I
brought you this. A top... A nice little humming
sound.

IRINA: It's magical.

MASHA: "A green oak stands by the sea,
A golden chain around it...
A golden chain around it..."
(With tears in her eyes) Why do I keep saying that?
I can't get it out of my head.

KULYGIN: There are thirteen at the table!

RODE: *(Loudly)* Don't tell me the schoolteacher's superstitious?!

(Laughter)

KULYGIN: Whenever there are thirteen at a table, it means that lovers are present. I think we should keep an eye on the doctor! *(Laughter)*

CHEBUTYKIN: I *am* a practiced sinner, but am I the only one who's noticed that Natasha's blushing?! *(Loud laughter;* NATASHA *runs out into the living room.* ANDREI *follows.)*

ANDREI: Don't pay any attention to them! Wait...please!... Don't go.

NATASHA: I'm so embarrassed.... I don't know what I did, they were all laughing at me. I know it's bad manners that I left the table, but I couldn't help myself.... I couldn't.... *(Covers her face with her hands)*

ANDREI: Natasha, please. Calm down, dear. They were only joking, they mean well. You dear little girl, listen to me—they are really very good people, and they do like you. Let's go over there, where they can't see.... *(Looks around)*

NATASHA: I'm not used to so many guests.

ANDREI: You are so young, so beautiful, and so young! Calm down, darling. Trust me, please trust me.... I'm so happy, I'm so much in love, I'm in ecstasy. They can't see us! They can't! Why did I fall in love with you? And when? I don't understand! Darling, my love—marry me. I love you, love you.... *(They kiss.)* ...as I have never loved anyone before....

(Two OFFICERS *enter, see the lovers kiss, and stare in astonishment.)*

END OF ACT ONE

ACT TWO

(The same. Around 8 p.m. We hear someone playing a concertina outside in the street. Dark. NATASHA enters, wearing a dressing gown, carrying a candle. She stops at the door to ANDREI's room.)

NATASHA: Andrei , Andruisha, what are you doing? Reading? Never mind, it's nothing.... *(Opens another door, looks in, closes it)* No candles are burning....

ANDREI: *(Coming out with a book)* What is it, Natasha?

NATASHA: Just seeing that there aren't any candles left burning. It's carnival week and the servants are simply beside themselves; I have to make sure something doesn't happen. Last night at midnight I was walking through the dining room and found a candle left burning. Who'd left it? I couldn't get a straight answer. *(Puts down her candle)* What time is it?

ANDREI: *(Looks at his watch)* A quarter past eight.

NATASHA: And Olga and Irina aren't even home yet. They work too hard, poor things. Olga at the teacher's council, Irina at that telegraph office...*(Sighs)* I told your sister this morning, "Irina, dear," I said, "you must take care of yourself." Doesn't listen to me. Did you say a quarter past eight? I'm worried that baby's not feeling well. Why is he so cold? Yesterday, he had a fever, and today he's cold.... I am getting worried.

ANDREI: There's nothing wrong with Bobik. The boy's fine.

NATASHA: Still, it's best to keep him on a diet. He's gotten me very worried. And the mummers are due after nine; it'd be better if they didn't come, Andrei.

ANDREI: I don't know.... They were invited. I really....

NATASHA: This morning when our little boy woke up and saw me, he suddenly smiled. That means he knew who I was. "Good morning, Bobik" I said. "Good morning, sweetheart." And he laughed. Babies know, they know. I'll tell them not to let the mummers in, dear.

ANDREI: *(Embarrassed)* Well... That's up to my sisters. This is their house.

NATASHA: They'll do what I wish. They're so sweet.... *(Going)* I gave orders that you're to have yogurt for supper. The doctor says it's yogurt and only yogurt or you'll never lose weight. *(Stops)* Bobik is so cold. I'm afraid it's the room. It would be nice if he had another room until the weather gets better. Say, Irina's; it's perfect for a baby, it gets a lot of sun. We should tell her she can share Olga's room.... It's not as if she were around all day, she only sleeps here. *(Pause)* Andrei, why don't you say something?

ANDREI: I was thinking.... There's nothing to say.

NATASHA: Yes.... There was something I was supposed to tell you.... I remember— Ferapont from the council office is here, he wants to see you.

ANDREI: *(Yawns)* Have him come in.

(NATASHA goes out. ANDREI reads his book, stooping over the candle she left behind. FERAPONT enters. He wears a tattered old coat with the collar turned up and earmuffs.)

ANDREI: Evening, old man. What's it this time?

FERAPONT: The Chairman sends this ledger and these papers. Here.... *(Hands them to him)*

ANDREI: *(Looking them over)* Thank you. Oh, right. Why couldn't you come earlier? It's past eight.

FERAPONT: What?

ANDREI: I said it's late. It's past eight.

FERAPONT: Yes, yes. When I got here the sun was still out, but they wouldn't let me in. They said you were busy. And if you're busy, you're busy. I'm in no hurry. *(Thinks* ANDREI *has asked something)* What?

ANDREI: Nothing. *(Looks through the ledger)* Tomorrow's Saturday. I'm supposed to have Saturdays off, but I'll come into the office anyway—to do some work. It's dull at home. *(Pause)* It's amazing, isn't it, old man, how life can suddenly turn against you, how it can cheat you. I picked up this book today—just out of boredom—some lectures from my university. I couldn't stop laughing. Look at me—secretary to the local district council, where Protopopov is chairman, and the most I have to look forward to is being made a member of the council. A local district council! Andrei Prozorov! The man who dreams night after night that he's a famous professor at Moscow University and the pride of all Russia!

FERAPONT: I wouldn't know.... I don't hear so good.

ANDREI: If you did, I don't suppose I'd be talking to you. I need to talk to someone; my wife doesn't understand me, and my sisters, I'm sort of afraid to talk to; I'm not sure why, perhaps I think they'd only laugh at me and make me feel ashamed of myself.... I don't drink, I don't enjoy going out with friends, but old man, what I wouldn't give to be sitting in the Tyestov right now or any other fine restaurant in Moscow!

FERAPONT: Moscow? The other day this contractor told me that's where some merchants or somebody

were eating pancakes; one ate forty and he died.
Maybe it was fifty, I forget.

ANDREI: You sit in those fine restaurants in Moscow
and not a soul do you know, and no one knows you,
yet not for a second do you feel like you don't belong.
And here, you know everyone, everyone knows you,
and you feel alone, a complete stranger.

FERAPONT: What? This same contractor said—though
he could have been lying—he said there was a rope
that stretched all the way across Moscow.

ANDREI: What for?

FERAPONT: I never asked. That's what he said, though.

ANDREI: Ridiculous. *(He reads.)* Ever been to Moscow?

FERAPONT: *(After a pause)* No. It was not God's will.
(Pause) Should I leave?

ANDREI: If you wish. God be with you. (FERAPONT
goes.) God be with you. *(Reading)* Come back
tomorrow and pick up these papers. Now run along.
(Looks up) He's already gone. *(A ring)* Yes, that's how
it goes. *(He stretches and slowly goes into his room. We
hear the nurse singing a lullaby to the baby.* MASHA *and*
VERSHININ *enter. While they talk a* MAID *lights the
candles and a lamp.)*

MASHA: I don't know. *(Pause)* I don't know. Of
course, habit accounts for part of it. For instance, after
Father's death it took us a long time to get used to the
orderlies not being around. But habit aside, I think
it's simply true. Maybe other towns are different, but
here the most refined and well-bred people are in the
military.

VERSHININ: My throat's dry. Could I have some tea?

MASHA: *(Looking at her watch)* They'll be bringing it
soon. I was married when I was eighteen, I was in

awe of my husband; he was a teacher and I was just
out of school. He seemed terribly wise and educated
and important. That has now changed, unfortunately.

VERSHININ: My...my...

MASHA: I didn't mean to talk about my husband, I
have grown used to him, but civilians in general so
often seem to be crude, coarse, and unsophisticated.
Rudeness offends me; it pains me. I suffer when I see
a man who isn't sufficiently refined or well-mannered
or polite. Just being around those other teachers who
work with my husband, it's simply torture.

VERSHININ: Yes.... But it seems to me...all the same...
the officers aren't any more interesting than the
civilians, in this town at any rate. Listen to either one
and all you'll hear is that he's sick of his wife, sick of
his house, sick of his job, sick of his horses.... Why is
it that we Russians are able to think the deepest
thoughts, and still end up living such shallow lives?
Why?

MASHA: Why?

VERSHININ: Why is he sick of his children, sick of his
wife? And why are his wife and children sick of him?

MASHA: You are in a glum mood today.

VERSHININ: Maybe. I haven't had dinner, I haven't
eaten all day. My daughter hasn't been feeling well
and whenever one of my girls is sick I get very
anxious and feel guilty for having given them such a
mother. I wish you had seen her today! What a pitiful
human being! We started arguing this morning at
seven, by nine I had slammed the door and walked
out. (Pause) I never talk about it, it's strange that I
would talk about it with you. (Kisses her hand) Don't
get angry. I don't have anyone but you, no one....
(Pause)

MASHA: The wind howling in the chimney. Just before Father died, there was a noise just like that in the chimney.

VERSHININ: Are you superstitious?

MASHA: Yes.

VERSHININ: Strange. *(Kisses her hand)* You are a charming, wonderful woman. Charming and wonderful! It's dark in here, but I can still see the sparkle in your eyes.

MASHA: *(Moving to another chair)* There's more light over here.

VERSHININ: I love you. I love you. I love your eyes, I love how you move. I dream about that.... You're charming and wonderful!

MASHA: *(Laughing gently)* It scares me when you talk like this. So why am I laughing? Please stop. Please. *(Softly)* No, talk. Why not?... *(Covers her face with her hands)* Why not? Someone's coming. Talk about something else....

(IRINA and TUZENBACH enter from the ballroom.)

TUZENBACH: In fact I have three last names: Tuzenbach-Krone-Altschauer, but still I'm as Russian as you are. There's nothing German about me—except perhaps a stubborn perseverance. I do walk you home every night.

IRINA: I'm exhausted!

TUZENBACH: And I'll keep on walking you home from the telegraph office for the next ten or twenty years—unless you tell me to stop. *(He sees MASHA and VERSHININ. Joyfully:)* Is that you? How are you?

IRINA: Home at last. *(To MASHA)* A woman came into the office today to send a telegram to her brother in Saratov that her son had died this morning. She

couldn't remember his address, so she just sent it to
Saratov, just to Saratov. She was crying. I don't know
why, but I was rude to her. "Look, I'm busy," I said.
So stupid!... Are we getting the mummers tonight?

MASHA: Yes.

IRINA: *(Sitting in an armchair)* I need to sit down.
I'm tired.

TUZENBACH: *(Smiling)* You look so small and helpless
when you come home from work.

(Pause)

IRINA: I'm exhausted. I don't like the telegraph office.
I don't like it.

MASHA: You've lost weight. *(Whistles a little)* And you
look younger, your face looks more like a boy's.

TUZENBACH: It's the way she does her hair.

IRINA: I have to find another job, this one isn't at all
right. It's not at all what I meant by work. It's without
poetry, without meaning.... *(A knock on the floor)* That's
the Doctor. *(To* TUZENBACH*)* Will you knock, dear? I
haven't the strength.... I'm exhausted.... *(*TUZENBACH
knocks.) He'll be up in a minute. Something has to be
done. The Doctor and Andrei played cards at the club
last night and lost again. Andrei, it seems, lost 200
rubles.

MASHA: *(With indifference)* What's done is done.

IRINA: Lost two weeks ago, lost in December. I wish
he'd hurry up and lose it all, then maybe we could
leave this town. Oh God, I dream of Moscow every
night! Is that crazy? *(Laughs)* Well, we'll be there in
June; still there's February, March, April, May...
almost half a year!

MASHA: Natasha shouldn't find out about Andrei
losing.

IRINA: I don't think she cares.

(CHEBUTYKIN, *having just gotten out of bed after a nap, comes into the living room. He combs his beard. He sits at the table and takes a newspaper from his pocket.*)

MASHA: Here he is.... Has he paid his rent yet?

IRINA: *(Laughs)* Nothing for eight months. Seems to have forgotten.

MASHA: *(Laughs)* He looks so self-important just sitting there....

(They all laugh.)

IRINA: Why so quiet, Alexander Ignatevich?

VERSHININ: I don't know. I have to have tea. My kingdom for a cup of tea! I haven't had anything since breakfast.

CHEBUTYKIN: Irina, my princess?

IRINA: What?

CHEBUTYKIN: Come here, please. Venez ici. *(*IRINA *goes and sits at the table.)* I need you beside me. *(*IRINA *begins to play solitaire.)*

VERSHININ: If there's not going to be any tea, then we might as well talk philosophy.

TUZENBACH: Yes, why not? What about?

VERSHININ: What about? Let's dream about...what life will be like after we're gone, say, in two or three hundred years.

TUZENBACH: Well? People will fly around in balloons, the cut of their coats will be different, perhaps a sixth sense will be discovered and even developed; but life itself will remain essentially the same, and that is—difficult, mysterious, and happy. Even after one thousand years, man will still be sighing—"Life is so hard!" Yet he'll still be just as afraid of dying, like us.

VERSHININ: *(Thoughtfully)* How can I put it? I'm convinced the world must and will change, little by little, as it is already changing right before our eyes. In two or three hundred years, say even a thousand—the actual length of time isn't what's important—a new and glorious age will begin. Of course, it will be too late for us, but we continue to live, to work...to suffer so that this age will come about. We are its creators; this fact is what gives meaning to our lives, and if you wish, our only happiness.

(MASHA *laughs softly.*)

TUZENBACH: What?

MASHA: I don't know. I've been laughing all day.

VERSHININ: Like you I went no further than cadet school; I didn't attend university. Yet I do read a lot, though quite indiscriminately. And no doubt I don't read everything that I should. Still, the older I get the more I want to know. My hair's getting gray, I'm almost an old man now, and I know so little, incredibly little. But there is one important truth, I think, I do understand, completely understand. And I just wish I could prove this to you, that for us today there can't be any happiness. There cannot and there should not!... Our fate is to struggle and only to struggle, leave happiness for those who will come later. *(Pause)* It's not for me; it's for my children's children, or for their children.

(FEDOTIK *and* RODE *come into the ballroom, sit, and sing softly, strumming on guitars.*)

TUZENBACH: So according to you, it's a waste of time to even look for happiness? But what if I told you I am happy?

VERSHININ: No.

TUZENBACH: *(Waves his hand and laughs)* Obviously, we don't understand each other. What can I say to convince you? *(MASHA laughs softly.)* Go ahead and laugh. *(To VERSHININ)* I don't care if it's two hundred, three hundred, or a million years, life won't be any different; it doesn't change; it follows its own laws, which have nothing to do with you, or at least which you will never fathom. Migrating birds, the cranes for example, fly and fly; what does it matter if they happen to have a profound or trivial thought in their heads, they still keep flying—and without knowing where or why. They fly and will continue to fly regardless of whether any philosophers are born into their flock; so let them talk philosophy if they wish, just as long as they don't stop flying....

MASHA: And the meaning?

TUZENBACH: The meaning.... Look, it's snowing. Where's the meaning in that? *(Pause)*

MASHA: It seems to me that a person must have faith or at least search for faith, or his life will be empty, just empty.... To be in this world and never know why cranes fly, why babies are born, why stars are in the night sky.... Either you know why you live or else everything becomes trivial and cheap. *(Pause)*

VERSHININ: Still it's a shame youth goes by.

MASHA: Gogol says: Life is boring!

TUZENBACH: And I say, it's impossible to argue with you people. Enough's enough.

CHEBUTYKIN: *(Reading)* Balzac was married in Berditchev. *(IRINA sings softly.)* I'll make a note. *(Does)* Balzac was married in Berditchev. *(Goes on reading)*

IRINA: *(Laying out the cards, thoughtfully)* Balzac was married in Berditchev.

TUZENBACH: *(To* MASHA*)* The die is cast. I've submitted my resignation.

MASHA: So I heard. What good will that do; I don't like civilians.

TUZENBACH: What's the difference?!...*(Gets up)* I'm not handsome, so what good am I as a soldier? In any event, it's no big thing.... I'm going to work. For once in my life I want to come home exhausted, crawl into bed and fall right to sleep. *(Going into the ballroom)* Workers, I'll bet, sleep like babies!

FEDOTIK: *(To* IRINA*)* I bought you these crayons from Pizhikov's shop. And this little penknife.

IRINA: You still think I'm a little girl. I have grown up. *(Takes the crayons and the knife, then with joy)* How cute!

FEDOTIK: And I bought this knife for me. Here, look—here's one blade, here's a second, here's a third, this is for ear wax, these are scissors, this for cleaning under your fingernails....

RODE: *(Loudly)* Doctor, how old are you really?

CHEBUTYKIN: Me? Thirty-two. *(Laughter)*

FEDOTIK: I'll show you another way to play solitaire. *(Lays out the cards)*

(A samovar is brought in; ANFISA *attends to it; a moment later,* NATASHA *enters and helps with the table;* SOLYONY *arrives, and after greetings, sits at the table.)*

VERSHININ: Listen to that wind!

MASHA: Yes. I'm fed up with winter. I think I've forgotten what summer's like.

IRINA: They're playing out. That means—we'll go to Moscow.

FEDOTIK: No. The eight is trapped under the two of spades. *(Laughs)* That means—no Moscow for you.

CHEBUTYKIN: *(Reading the paper)* Smallpox epidemic in China.

ANFISA: *(Approaching* MASHA*)* Masha, have some tea, dear.... *(To* VERSHININ*)* And you too, Sir. Excuse me, but I forgot your name.

MASHA: Bring it here. I won't go there.

IRINA: Anfisa!

ANFISA: I'm coming. I'm coming.

NATASHA: *(To* SOLYONY*)* Babies know, they just do. I said—"Good morning, Bobik! Good morning, sweetheart!" and he looked up at me with the most unusual look on his face. Don't think I'm saying this because I'm his mother, really that's not why. He's a very unique child.

SOLYONY: If this baby were mine, I'd have fried him in a pan and eaten him.

(Takes his glass into the living room and sits in a corner)

NATASHA: *(Covering her face with her hands)* What a rude, vulgar man!

MASHA: Blessed is he who does not notice whether it's summer or winter. In Moscow, I think I wouldn't ever notice the weather.

VERSHININ: A couple of days ago I was reading through a diary a French cabinet minister kept while in prison. He was in there because of the Panama scandal. He writes with such joy, such delight about the birds he saw through his cell window. The same birds he'd never even noticed as a cabinet minister. Of course, now that he's out, he's forgotten the birds again. That's what will happen to you, once you get to

Moscow—you won't even notice that you're there. We're never happy, we only hope to be happy.

TUZENBACH: *(Takes a box from the table)* What happened to all the candy?

IRINA: Ask Solyony.

TUZENBACH: He ate the whole box?

ANFISA: *(Serving tea)* This letter is for you, Sir.

VERSHININ: For me? Yes. *(Takes the letter)* From my daughter. *(Reads)* My, my, of course.... I'll go quietly. Excuse me. I won't have any tea. *(Stands up, excited)* It never stops....

MASHA: What is it? Can't you tell me?

VERSHININ: *(Quietly)* My wife has taken poison again. I have to go. I'll just leave. How unpleasant. *(Kisses MASHA's hand)* My dear, kind, decent woman.... I'll let myself out, quietly. *(Exits)*

ANFISA: Where's he going? I just served him tea.... Such people...

MASHA: *(Angrily)* Will you be quiet?! You never stop babbling! *(Goes to the table)* I'm getting tired of you, old woman!

ANFISA: Why are you angry? Dear!

ANDREI: *(Off)* Anfisa!

ANFISA: *(Mimicking)* "Anfisa! Anfisa!" You'd think he didn't have two legs. *(She exits.)*

MASHA: *(In the ballroom, by the table, angrily)* Do you have to take up the whole table?! *(Pushes the cards away)* Play over there. Drink your tea!

IRINA: Masha, why are you behaving like this?

MASHA: If you don't like the way I behave then don't speak to me. Leave me alone.

CHEBUTYKIN: *(Laughing)* Leave her alone, leave her alone.

MASHA: You're sixty and you act like you're two, please just keep your damn mouth closed!

NATASHA: Need you use such language, dear? With that face and figure, there's no telling what a mark you could make in society; frankly, it's your language that keeps you back. Je vous prie, pardonnez-moi, Marie, mais vous avez des manieres un peu grossieres.

TUZENBACH: *(Holding back his laughter)* Could I... Could I.... The brandy, quick.

NATASHA: Il parait, que mon Bobik déjà ne dort pas. He's awake. He hasn't been feeling well today. I better look in on him. Excuse me.... *(Exits)*

IRINA: Where did Alexander Ignatevich go?

MASHA: Home. His wife keeps doing the most extraordinary things.

TUZENBACH: *(Goes to SOLYONY with the brandy flask)* You go on sitting there; God knows what goes on in your mind. Here—let's call a truce. Let's have some brandy. *(They drink.)* I suppose they'll make me play the piano all night. And the most ridiculous tunes... Well, that's life!

SOLYONY: Why a truce? I haven't fought with you.

TUZENBACH: But you always make me feel like we have. I have to admit you're a pretty strange person.

SOLYONY: *(Declaims)* "Yes I am strange, this I confess, But who is not, in this God's great mess!" —"Don't be angry, Aleko!"

TUZENBACH: Aleko? What does Aleko have to do with anything? *(Pause)*

SOLYONY: When it's just me and somebody else, I'm fine, I behave like anyone else. It's crowds, they make me nervous, so I say stupid things. But I'm more honest and decent than many people. And I can prove it.

TUZENBACH: You've certainly irked me often enough. And why do you always pick on me? Still, for some reason, I like you. I'm getting drunk tonight. What the hell. Have a drink.

SOLYONY: You too. *(They drink.)* I've nothing against you, Baron. But I have the temperament of Lermontov. *(Whispers)* I'm told I even look like Lermontov.

TUZENBACH: I've sent in my resignation. Enough said! I've been thinking about it for five years. Now I've done it. I will work.

SOLYONY: "Don't be angry, Aleko... Forget, forget, thy dream of long ago..."

(ANDREI enters.)

TUZENBACH: I will work.

CHEBUTYKIN: *(Going with* IRINA *into the ballroom)* And then the food, authentic Caucasian onion soup, and for the meat dish, chekhartma.

SOLYONY: Cheremsha's not meat. It's a plant. Like an onion.

CHEBUTYKIN: I beg to disagree. Chekhartma is not like an onion it is rather like roast lamb.

SOLYONY: I'm telling you it's like an onion.

CHEBUTYKIN: And I'm telling you it's like lamb!

SOLYONY: An onion!

CHEBUTYKIN: How do you know? You've never even been to the Caucasus, and you've never eaten chekhartma!

SOLYONY: I've never eaten it, because I hate it. It smells like onion!

ANDREI: Please, please gentlemen! That's enough!

TUZENBACH: What time are the mummers coming?

IRINA: They said around nine. So any minute now.

TUZENBACH: *(Embraces* ANDREI; *singing a folk song:)* "Oh what a house. Oh what a house! What a house I built for me!"

ANDREI: *(Sings and dances)* "And when it rains. And when it rains."

CHEBUTYKIN: *(Dancing)* "Inside is like the sea!"

TUZENBACH: *(Kisses* ANDREI*)* What the hell, let's drink. Andrei, my good friend, to you! And I'm going with you when you go, to Moscow, to the university.

SOLYONY: Which one? There are two universities in Moscow.

ANDREI: There's only one university in Moscow.

SOLYONY: No. Two.

ANDREI: Who knows, maybe there are three. The more the merrier!

SOLYONY: There are two universities in Moscow! *(Murmurs and hushes)* There are two universities in Moscow. The old one and the new one. But if you don't want to listen, if I'm annoying you, just say so, I can shut up. I can even go to another room. *(He goes.)*

TUZENBACH: Bravo! Bravo! *(Laughs)* You've twisted my arm, I'm going to play the piano. Funny man, Solyony.... *(Goes to the piano and plays a waltz)*

MASHA: *(Dancing alone)* Baron's drunk! Baron's drunk! Baron's drunk!

(NATASHA comes in.)

NATASHA: *(To CHEBUTYKIN)* Ivan Romanich!

(She whispers something to him, then goes out quietly. CHEBUTYKIN touches TUZENBACH on the shoulder and whispers something to him.)

IRINA: What is it?

CHEBUTYKIN: Time to go. Goodnight.

TUZENBACH: Goodnight. It's time we went.

IRINA: But what about the mummers?

ANDREI: *(Confused)* There won't be any mummers. You see, dear, Natasha says Bobik isn't feeling well, and so...well...don't look at me.... It's all the same to me....

IRINA: Bobik isn't feeling well.

MASHA: Damnit, the nerve! But if we're thrown out, we're thrown out. *(To IRINA)* Bobik isn't the one who's sick. It's her.... Here! *(Points to her head)* Vulgar petty bourgeois.

(ANDREI goes into his room, CHEBUTYKIN follows. In the ballroom they are saying good-byes.)

FEDOTIK: A pity. I was looking forward to tonight. But—if the baby isn't well.... I'll bring him some toys tomorrow.

RODE: *(Loudly)* And I was expecting to dance all night! That's why I napped all afternoon. It's only nine o'clock.

MASHA: Let's go outside. We can decide what to do out there.

(Short interlude. Good-byes are heard. TUZENBACH's *merry laughter is heard. All go out.* ANFISA *and the* MAID *clear the table, and put out the candles. The nurse sings.* ANDREI, *wearing an overcoat and hat, and* CHEBUTYKIN *enter silently.)*

CHEBUTYKIN: I never had the time to marry. Life flashed by me like lightning. Besides, I was madly in love with your mother, and she was already married.

ANDREI: A man shouldn't get married, it's boring.

CHEBUTYKIN: Maybe. But what about being left alone, my friend? Loneliness. It's a terrible thing.... But yes—I guess it's all the same.

ANDREI: We should hurry.

CHEBUTYKIN: What for? We still have time.

ANDREI: I'm afraid my wife will stop me.

CHEBUTYKIN: Ah!

ANDREI: I'm not going to gamble tonight; just sit and watch. I don't feel so well.... What should I take for my asthma, Doctor?

CHEBUTYKIN: Don't ask me. I don't remember, anything, I don't know.

ANDREI: Let's go out through the kitchen. *(They go out. A bell rings twice. Voices and laughter are heard.)*

IRINA: *(Entering)* Who is it?

ANFISA: *(Whispers)* The mummers! *(Bell)*

IRINA: Tell them no one's home. Apologize. (ANFISA *goes out.* IRINA *walks about the room deep in thought. She is excited.* SOLYONY *enters.)*

SOLYONY: *(Surprised)* No one's here. Where'd they go?

IRINA: Home.

SOLYONY: Strange. Then you're alone?

IRINA: Alone. *(Pause)* Goodnight.

SOLYONY: My behavior tonight was thoughtless... boarish. But you're not like the others, you are kind and pure, you see the truth.... You alone can understand me. I love you so much. I can't tell you how much I love you.

IRINA: Goodnight! Go away.

SOLYONY: I can't live without you. *(Follows her)* You are my happiness! *(Through tears)* What eyes! What marvelous glorious eyes! No other woman on earth has such eyes....

IRINA: *(Coldly)* Stop it, Vassily Vassilych!

SOLYONY: It's the first time I have talked to you of my love. I feel as if I'm not on the earth, but another planet. *(Rubs his forehead)* Never mind. Of course, I can't force you to love me...but I won't stand back and watch anyone else take my place...I won't... I swear to God I'll kill anyone who even tries.... How wonderful you are! So wonderful!

(NATASHA enters with a candle; she looks in through one door, then another, passing ANDREI's door.)

NATASHA: Andrei's in there. I'll let him read. Oh, excuse me, Vassily Vassilych, I didn't know you were still here. I'm all dressed for bed.

SOLYONY: Goodnight. *(He goes.)*

NATASHA: You look so tired, dear! *(Kisses her)* You should have gone to bed early.

IRINA: Is the baby asleep?

NATASHA: Yes, but just barely. Oh, I meant to tell you earlier—but you must have been out or maybe I was busy.... I think Bobik's room is too cold for him. Your room would be perfect for the child. My dear, would you please move into Olga's room for a while?

IRINA: *(Confused, not understanding)* Where?

NATASHA: You and Olga can share her room, just for now, dear, and Bobik can have yours. He's such a darling; today I said, "Bobik, you're mine! All mine!" And he looked up at me with his cute little eyes. *(A bell)* That must be Olga. And look at the time!

(Maid enters and whispers to NATASHA.)

NATASHA: Protopopov? What a funny man. Protopopov's come to take me for a ride in his troika. *(Laughs)* Men do the strangest things.... *(A bell rings)* Now who's that? I suppose I'll go for a half an hour.... *(To the maid)* Tell him I'll be right there. *(Bell)* Now maybe that's Olga. *(Leaves; the maid runs out.)*

(IRINA sits, deep in thought. KULYGIN and OLGA enter, followed by VERSHININ.)

KULYGIN: There you are. I thought we were having a party.

VERSHININ: Strange. I wasn't gone that long, half an hour or so. They were expecting the mummers....

IRINA: Everyone's gone.

KULYGIN: Masha too? Where'd she go? And why is Protopopov outside in his troika? Who's he waiting for?

IRINA: Don't ask questions.... I'm exhausted.

KULYGIN: So touchy!

OLGA: My meeting just got over. I'm so tired. The headmistress was sick, so I had to take her place. I have such a headache.... *(Sits)* Andrei lost 200 rubles yesterday.... The whole town's talking about it.

KULYGIN: The meeting tired me out too.*(Sits)*

VERSHININ: My wife tried to poison herself again.
To pay me back for something or other I did, I guess.
She's all right now. I just want to relax.... But on
second thought maybe we shouldn't stay. Come on,
Fyodor Ilych, let's you and I go somewhere. I can't,
I just can't go home. Come on.

KULYGIN: I'm tired. Not tonight. *(Gets up)* I'm tired.
Did my wife go home?

IRINA: I suppose so.

KULYGIN: *(Kisses* IRINA*'s hand)* Goodnight. I'm going
to do nothing but relax tomorrow, and the day after
tomorrow. *(Going)* What I really wanted was a cup
of tea. I was looking forward to this evening—O,
fallacem hominum spem! For exclamations, it's the
accusative case....

VERSHININ: I'll go by myself then.

(They exit, with KULYGIN *whistling.)*

OLGA: My head...such a headache... Andrei's been
losing money.... The whole town's talking.... I'm going
to bed. *(Going)* Tomorrow I have off. God, what a
relief. I'm free tomorrow, I'm free the day after
tomorrow.... Oh my head, my head.... *(Exits)*

IRINA: *(Alone)* Everyone's gone. Nobody's left.

(A concertina is heard from the street. The nurse sings.)

NATASHA: *(In fur coat and cap, moving across the
ballroom, followed by the maid.)* I'll be back in half an
hour. I'm going for a little ride. *(Exits)*

IRINA: *(Alone in her misery)* To Moscow! Moscow!
Moscow!

END OF ACT TWO

ACT THREE

(The room shared by OLGA *and* IRINA. *Beds are screened off, left and right. A little after two in the morning We hear the fire alarm; it has been ringing for quite some time. No one in the house has gone to bed.* MASHA *lies on a sofa, dressed as usual in black.* OLGA *and* ANFISA *enter.)*

ANFISA: They're now huddled under the stairs. I said to them, "Come up, children." I said, "You can't go on like this." They start crying: "Where's our father?" They said, "What if he got burned up?" Think of it! People are in the yard too...also with hardly any clothes on.

OLGA: *(Taking a dress out of the closet)* Take this gray dress...and this...the blouse too... And the skirt... My God, it's awful isn't it? Almost all of Kirsanovsky street burned.... Take this...this... *(Throws clothes into her hands)* The poor Vershinin children are in shock.... Their house just escaped.... We must put them up tonight.... We can't let them go back there.... And poor Fedotik's lost everything. He's nothing left.

ANFISA: Dear, I can't carry all this.... You'll have to call Ferapont.

OLGA: *(Rings)* They'll never answer. *(Goes to the door)* Come here! Anyone! *(Through the open door we see a window aglow with the fire; a fire engine is heard passing the house.)* It's so awful. It's sickening.

(FERAPONT enters.)

OLGA: Take all these down.... The Kolotilin children are under the stairs.... Give them these. Pass these out. This too...

FERAPONT: Yes Ma'am. In 1812 Moscow burned down. And, oh God, weren't those Frenchmen surprised!

OLGA: Go on, go on!

FERAPONT: Yes Ma'am. *(Goes)*

OLGA: Anfisa, dear, give them whatever we have. We don't need anything. Give it all to them... I can hardly stand up, I'm so tired.... We can't let the Vershinins go back there.... The girls can sleep in the living room. The Colonel downstairs in the Baron's apartment. And Fedotik too—no, maybe the ballroom. The Doctor's drunk, terribly, drunk, as if on purpose; we can't put anyone in with him.... Vershinin's wife—with her girls in the living room.

ANFISA: *(Tired)* Olga dear, don't throw me out! Please don't!

OLGA: Don't talk nonsense, no one's throwing you out.

ANFISA: *(Puts OLGA's head against her breast)* Olga, my little girl, I work, I work hard.... I just get weak, and that's when they say..."Get out!" Where will I go? Where? I'm over eighty.... Almost eighty-two.

OLGA: Sit down...you're tired, poor dear. *(Makes her sit)* Rest. You do look pale.

(NATASHA enters.)

NATASHA: They say a committee to assist the victims of the fire must be formed at once. Well, I think it's a wonderful idea. The poor must be helped. This is the duty of the rich. Can you believe Bobik and Sofichka slept through the whole fire? And with all the people

here, the house is full of them, you can't move
without stepping on someone. A flu's been going
around in town. I'm afraid the children will catch it.

OLGA: *(Not listening to her)* We can't see the fire from
in here. It's peaceful here....

NATASHA: Yes.... My hair must look terrible. *(In front
of the mirror)* I've been told I've been putting on
weight. Well, that's not true. Not true at all... Masha's
asleep, the poor dear...she's exhausted.... *(Coldly, to
ANFISA)* Don't you dare sit down in my presence!
Get up! Get out of this room! *(ANFISA leaves. Pause.)*

NATASHA: I don't understand why you keep that old
woman.

OLGA: *(Embarrassed)* I'm sorry, but I don't understand
how...you just....

NATASHA: She's of no use here. She's a peasant. She
should be in a village somewhere.... Why spoil them?
I like order in a house. I can't have people just taking
up room. *(Caresses her cheek)* You are tired, poor thing.
Our headmistress is tired. When Sofichka grows up
and goes to your school, I'll be so frightened of you.

OLGA: I'm not going to be headmistress.

NATASHA: Of course you are, Olga. It's all settled.

OLGA: I'll refuse the job. I couldn't...I don't have the
strength.... *(Drinks a glass of water)* You were so rude
to Anfisa just now.... I'm sorry, but I can't stand that....
Everything suddenly went dark....

NATASHA: *(Excited)* Forgive me, Olga, forgive me....
I didn't mean to upset you. *(MASHA gets up, takes a
pillow, and goes out angrily.)*

OLGA: Try to understand, dear... perhaps we were
brought up in a strange way, but I can't stand such

things. That kind of behavior only depresses me,
I get ill... I simply lose strength.

NATASHA: Forgive me, forgive me... *(Kisses her)*

OLGA: Even the slightest rudeness, the least impolite
word, hurts me.

NATASHA: I can be a bit blunt sometimes, it's true,
but you have to admit, dear, she'd be better off in
some village.

OLGA: She's been with us for thirty years.

NATASHA: But she can't work anymore. Either I don't
understand you, or you don't want to understand me.
She can't work, she only sleeps and sits.

OLGA: So let her sit!

NATASHA: *(Surprised)* What do you mean, let her sit?
She's a servant. *(Through tears)* I can't understand you,
Olga. I have a wet nurse, a governess, we have a
maid, a cook.... What do we need this old woman for?
What good is she?

(Fire alarm is heard)

OLGA: I've aged ten years tonight.

NATASHA: It's time we got one thing settled, Olga.
You have the school, I have the home. You teach your
students, I run this house. And when it comes to the
servants, I know what I'm talking about. I know what
I'm talking about.... And tomorrow that old thief, that
hag, goes! *(Stomping)* That bitch! And don't you dare
fight me. Don't you dare!... Really, if you don't move
somewhere I swear we'll never stop fighting. This
can't go on.

*(*KULGYIN* enters.)*

KULYGIN: Where's Masha? It's time we went home.
The fire looks like it's burning out. *(Stretches himself)*

With that wind, at first it seemed the whole town would go. *(Sits)* I'm tired. Dear Olga.... Often I think if it hadn't been for Masha, I'd have married you. You are very kind.... I'm absolutely exhausted. *(Listens)*

OLGA: What is it?

KULYGIN: The Doctor. He's been drinking— obviously. He's terribly drunk. *(Gets up)* Sounds like he's coming up here. Do you hear him? Yes, here.... *(Laughs to himself)* That man... incredible... I think I'll hide and scare him. *(Goes to a corner, behind the wardrobe)* What an old rascal.

OLGA: He hasn't touched a drop in two years, and he goes and picks tonight....

(Goes with NATASHA *to the back of the room.* CHEBUTYKIN *enters, acting sober. He stops, looks around, then goes to the wash stand and begins to wash his hands.)*

CHEBUTYKIN: *(Morose)* To hell with all of them...to hell.... They think I'm a doctor, can cure everything, but I know absolutely nothing. Forgotten everything I ever knew, I remember nothing, nothing. (OLGA *and* NATASHA *leave, unnoticed by him.)* To hell with them! Last Wednesday I treated a woman in the Zasypi slums and she died, and it's my fault that she died. Yes...I did know a few things some twenty-five years ago, now I can't remember anything. Nothing... Maybe I'm not even a man; maybe I'm just pretending to have arms, legs, head. Maybe I don't exist; it only seems like I walk, eat, sleep. *(He is crying.)* If only that were true. *(Stops crying, morosely)* Hell knows.... The other day they were talking in the club; they were saying— Shakespeare, Voltaire.... Never read them, but made a face like I did. The others did too, just like me. Cheap! Mean! And that woman I let die on Wednesday, I thought of her...it all came back to me,

and I felt like filth, rankness, and waste.... Went out
and got drunk....

(IRINA, VERSHININ *and* TUZENBACH *enter, then*
KULYGIN; TUZENBACH *now wears new and fashionable
civilian clothes.*)

IRINA: Let's sit here. No one will come in here.

VERSHININ: If it weren't for the soldiers, the whole
town would have gone up. Good men! *(Rubs his
hands appreciatively)* Heroic! What a fine bunch!

KULYGIN: *(Coming up to him)* What time is it?

TUZENBACH: It's almost four. It's getting light.

IRINA: They're all sitting downstairs, no one seems to
be thinking of leaving. Your friend, Solyony, is down
there too. *(To* CHEBUTYKIN*)* Shouldn't you be getting
to bed, Doctor?

CHEBUTYKIN: Nothing...thank you.... *(Combs his beard)*

KULYGIN: *(Laughs)* Found some spirits to commune
with, have you, Doctor? *(Pats him on the back)* Good
man! Heroic! *In vino veritas,* as the ancients used to
say.

TUZENBACH: They keep asking me to arrange a
concert to aid the victims.

IRINA: Well, but who can....

TUZENBACH: It could be arranged, if we wanted to.
Take Masha... In my opinion, she is an excellent
pianist.

KULYGIN: Yes, excellent!

IRINA: She's forgotten everything. She hasn't played
in three years, four years....

TUZENBACH: No one in this town understands
the least bit about music, not one person, but I, I

understand and I can assure you that Masha plays beautifully; I would say she has true talent.

KULYGIN: I agree, Baron. I love her very much. She's wonderful, Masha.

TUZENBACH: Imagine! To have such talent while knowing there's no one, not a soul, to appreciate it!

KULYGIN: *(Sighs)* Yes...though I wonder if it's something a woman should be seen doing, in public, I mean. *(Pause)* You see, I don't know. Perhaps it will be all right. Of course, our principal's a terribly kind and understanding man, even if he is a bit old-fashioned.... Of course, it's none of his business, but I think it only polite to ask him first.

(CHEBUTYKIN *takes a porcelain clock into his hands and examines it.*)

VERSHININ: I'm covered in soot from the fire; I must look a mess. *(Pause)* I heard a rumor yesterday that the brigade's being transferred somewhere far away. Some say...Siberia. Some say—Poland.

TUZENBACH: I heard that too. Well, if it's true, the town will be empty.

IRINA: Then we'll leave too!

(CHEBUTYKIN *drops the clock, which breaks.*)

CHEBUTYKIN: To smithereens! *(Pause. Everyone is confused.)*

KULYGIN: *(Picking up the pieces)* That was an expensive clock! Oh, Doctor, you should have your hand slapped for that.

IRINA: That's Mother's clock.

CHEBUTYKIN: Maybe... If it's hers, it's hers.... Maybe I didn't really break it, it only seems like I did. Maybe it only seems to us that we exist, but we don't. I don't know anything, no one does. *(At the door)* What are you staring at? Natasha is having a little affair with Protopopov, and you don't see that....You sit there, you see nothing, and Natasha is having a little affair with Protopopov.... *(Singing)* "How would you like this plum from me?..." *(He leaves.)*

VERSHININ: My, my. *(Laughs)* It's all strange. *(Pause)* When the fire broke out, I ran home.... I come up to my house and look—our house is safe, untouched, and out of danger, but my two little girls are standing on the steps, in only their underwear, their mother isn't with them, people are panicking, horses, dogs run wild, and my little girls' faces show such fear, horror, helplessness, God knows what else. Their faces were enough to break my heart. My God, I thought, how much more suffering will these girls have to endure in their lives! I grab them, run, while still thinking the same thought: How much suffering will they have to endure in this world! *(Fire alarm; pause)* I come here, their mother is here, she's angry and she's yelling.

(MASHA enters with a pillow and sits on the sofa.)

VERSHININ: And when my little girls were standing on those steps, and the street was turning redder and redder, and all this awful noise, I imagined that this was how it must have been many years ago as an army attacked, then looted, then burned.... Yet there's such a profound difference between then and now! And given a little more time, say two or three hundred years, no doubt our age will be held in much the same contempt as we now hold the past; and looked back upon as clumsy, thick, filthy, and alien. Yes, indeed, what a life there will be, what a life! *(Laughs)* Forgive me, I've drifted off into philosophy again. Please, humor me, I'm longing to talk philosophy, I'm just in the mood. *(Pause)* It seems like everyone's asleep. As I was saying: What a life it will be! Just imagine.... So today there are only three like you in this town, but given time there will be more, and more, and more.... And a time will come when everything will be changed, and it's your sensibilities which this town will then reflect; then even those like you will be outdated, and people will be born who are better than you.... *(Laughs)* My, my, what a strange mood I'm in today. I feel this great desire to live! *(Sings)* "All men should once with love grow tender, All men must once to love surrender."

MASHA: Tra-ta-ta?

VERSHININ: Tra-ta-ta....

MASHA: Tra-ra-ram-tam-tam?

VERSHININ: Tra-ra-ram-tam-tam. *(Laughs)*

(FEDOTIK *enters.*)

FEDOTIK: *(Dancing)* Ashes! Ashes! It's all ashes! *(Laughter)*

IRINA: I don't find that funny. Is everything burned?

FEDOTIK: *(Laughs)* Of course. Not a thing is left. The guitar's burned, the photographs are burned, all my letters.... And the notebook I was going to give you as a present, that's burned too.

(SOLYONY *comes in.*)

IRINA: No, you can't come in here, Vassily Vassilych. Please go away.

SOLYONY: How come the Baron can come here and I can't?

VERSHININ: We really should go. How's the fire?

SOLYONY: They say it's dying down. Now, really, I find it strange that the Baron can and I can't.

VERSHININ: Tra-ra-ram-tam-tam?

MASHA: Tra-ra-ram-tam-tam.

VERSHININ: *(Laughs to* SOLYONY*)* Let's go downstairs.

SOLYONY: Very well, but I've made a note of this.
"My point is made, no clearer can it be,
So now let the geese wait and see."
(To TUZENBACH*)* Cluck-cluck-cluck.

(Goes out with VERSHININ *and* FEDOTIK.*)*

IRINA: Solyony filled the room with smoke.
(In surprise) The Baron's asleep! Baron! Baron!

TUZENBACH: *(Waking)* I must be very tired.... The
brickworks... No, I'm not talking in my sleep, I'm
serious; I'm taking a job at the brickworks.... I've
talked to them. *(Tenderly, to* IRINA*)* You're so pale,
beautiful, and enchanting.... Like a light shining in the
dark.... You are sad, disappointed with life.... Come
with me, let's get away and work together!

MASHA: Nikolai Lvovich, I think you should leave.

TUZENBACH: *(Laughs)* So you're here. I didn't see you.
(Kisses IRINA*'s hand)* Good night, I'm going.... To look
at you now, it seems so long since your birthday party
when you were so happy speaking about the joys of
work.... Life seemed happy then to me too! Where has
it all gone? *(Kisses her hand)* You have tears in your
eyes. Get some sleep; it's getting light.... Morning is
coming.... Given the chance, I would give my life for
you!

MASHA: Nikolai Lvovich, will you go? Really—

TUZENBACH: I'm gone. *(Exits)*

MASHA: *(Lies down)* Are you asleep, Fyodor?

KULYGIN: Huh?

MASHA: Shouldn't you go home?

KULYGIN: Dear Masha, dear sweet Masha....

IRINA: She's tired. Maybe you should let her rest, Fyodor.

KULYGIN: I'll go. My good, lovely wife.... I love you, only you....

MASHA: *(Angrily)* Amo, amas, amat, amamus, amatis, amant.

KULYGIN: *(Laughs)* She's wonderful, isn't she? These past seven years have flown by, it seems like only yesterday we were married. It's true, it does. You really are wonderful. I'm content, content, content.

MASHA: Bored, bored, bored. *(Sits up)* I can't stop thinking about it.... It's simply outrageous. It's been eating at me all day.... I can't keep quiet. I'm talking about Andrei.... He's mortgaged the house...and his wife got a hold of the money, but this house doesn't belong just to him, it's ours too.

KULYGIN: Why go into that, Masha? Andrei's deep in debt, God help him.

MASHA: I still think it's outrageous. *(Lies down)*

KULYGIN: It's not as if we're poor. I work; I have my classes, my private lessons.... I'm a simple, honest man.... *Omnia mea mecum porto*, as they say.

MASHA: I don't want anything, but it's just so unfair, it's disgusting. *(Pause)* You go, Fyodor.

KULYGIN: *(Kisses her)* You're tired, rest here for a half an hour, I'll sit downstairs and wait. Sleep.... *(Going)* I'm content, I'm content, I'm content. *(Goes)*

IRINA: It's true, all that's left of our brother is the shell; he's become so weak and old and petty living with this woman! It is true—he used to dream of being a professor, and yesterday I heard him bragging about finally being made a member of the local district

council. He's a member, Protopopov is chairman....
The whole town's laughing about it. He's the only one
who doesn't know, and doesn't see.... Everyone runs
to the fire, he stays alone in his room and plays his
violin. *(Nervously)* It's awful, awful, awful. *(Cries)*
I can't, I can't stand it anymore!... I can't, I can't!

(OLGA comes in and begins to put her little table in order.
IRINA *is sobbing.)*

IRINA: Throw me out, throw me out, I can't stand it!

OLGA: *(Alarmed)* What is it? What is it, dear?

IRINA: *(Sobbing)* Where? Where has it all gone? Where
is it? My God, oh my God! I've forgotten everything,
everything... I don't remember the Italian for window,
or, or ceiling.... I forget everything, every day I forget
more, and life keeps passing and it's never coming
back, and we'll never go to Moscow.... I know we'll
never go....

OLGA: Dear, dear....

IRINA: *(Trying to control herself)* God, I'm unhappy....
I can't work. I won't work. Enough, enough! I tried
the telegraph office, now I'm at the town hall, and I
only have hate and contempt for the work they have
me do.... I'm already nearly twenty-four years old,
I've been working for ages, my brain's dried up,
I've become skinny, plain, old, and I have nothing,
nothing, nothing to feel good about, and days keep
passing and it seems that I'm drifting away from
the real and beautiful life, getting farther and farther
away, like I'm going down a hole. I'm in despair,
I'm in despair! I can't understand why I'm still alive,
why I haven't killed myself.

OLGA: Don't cry, you dear little girl, don't cry....
It hurts me.

IRINA: I'm not crying, I'm not.... Enough.... See, I'm not crying anymore. Enough...enough!

OLGA: Dear, if you want the advice of a sister and a friend, marry the Baron. (IRINA *cries softly.*) I know you respect him, you think very highly of him.... He may not be handsome, but he is honest, decent.... Women don't marry out of love, but out of duty. At least that's what I think, and I know I would marry a man without loving him. Whoever he was, I would marry him, as long as he was kind. He could even be old....

IRINA: I've always been waiting for us to move to Moscow; that's where I'll meet the man I would love; I used to dream of him, and love him.... But that's all turned out to be nonsense, just nonsense....

OLGA: *(Embraces her sister)* My dear beautiful sister, I understand everything, after the Baron resigned and showed up here in his civilian clothes, he looked so ugly, I just cried. "What are you crying about?" he asks. How could I tell him! But if God wants you to marry him, I would be happy. That's different, quite different.

(NATASHA, *with a candle, walks the stage without speaking.*)

MASHA: *(Sitting up)* She skulks around as if she'd started the fire.

OLGA: You are stupid, Masha. You're the stupidest one in the family. I'm sorry, but I had to say that. *(Pause)*

MASHA: I have a confession to make to the both of you. I'm burning up inside. I'll confess to you, but never again to anyone else.... I'm going to tell you now. *(Softly)* It's my secret, but you have to know it.... I have to tell someone.... *(Pause)* I love, I love...I love a man...he was just here.... Why can't I just say it?... In a word—I love Vershinin.

OLGA: *(Goes behind the screen)* Stop it! I'm not going to listen!

MASHA: What am I going to do? *(Takes her head in her hands)* At first he just seemed strange, then I began feeling sorry for him.... Then I fell in love with him, just as he is... with his voice, his words, his miseries, his two daughters.

OLGA: *(Behind the screen)* I'm not listening. You can say all the stupid things you want, but I won't listen!

MASHA: Oh, Olga, you're the stupid one. I am in love—and that's to be my fate, my lot in life.... And he loves me.... It's all so awful.... It isn't right, is it? *(Takes IRINA's hand and draws her to her)* My dear.... What are we going to do with our lives, what's going to happen to us?....You read about love in a novel and it all seems so old and obvious, but when it happens to you, you realize no one knows anything.... We have to decide for ourselves.... Dear ones, dear sisters... I've confessed, now I'll keep quiet.... Like Gogol's madman, I'll keep quiet...keep quiet....

(ANDREI enters, followed by FERAPONT.)

ANDREI: *(Angrily)* Just what do you want? I don't understand.

FERAPONT: *(At the door, impatiently)* I've already told you ten times, Andrei Sergeevich.

ANDREI: In the first place it's not Andrei Sergheevich; it's "Sir" to you.

FERAPONT: The firemen, Sir, want to know if they can cut across your garden to get to the river. If not they have to go all the way around, all the way around; it's a nuisance.

ANDREI: All right. Tell them it's all right.

(FERAPONT *leaves*.)

ADREI: I'm sick and tired of them. Where's Olga?

(OLGA *comes out of the closet*.)

ANDREI: I need the key to the cabinet. I lost mine.
It's the little one.

(OLGA *gives him the key;* IRINA *goes behind the screen.*
Pause.)

ANDREI: Why are you so quiet, Olga? *(Pause)* Look,
I've just about had it with this stupid sulking. There's
no reason for it....You here too, Masha. And Irina as
well. Good, since we're all here, let's get something
out in the open. What do you have against me? What?

OLGA: Not now, Andrei dear, please. We'll talk
tomorrow. What an exhausting night!

ANDREI: *(Confused)* Don't get upset. I'm asking very
calmly what do you have against me? Tell me the
truth.

VERSHININ: *(Off)* Tra-ra-ram-tam-tam!

MASHA: *(Stands; loudly)* Tra-ta-ta! *(To* OLGA*)*
Goodnight, Olga, God bless you. *(Goes behind the
screen and kisses* IRINA*)* Sleep well... Goodnight,
Andrei. Go now, they're tired.... You can talk
tomorrow.... *(She leaves.)*

OLGA: This can wait until tomorrow, Andrei.
(Goes behind the screen) It's time to go to bed.

ANDREI: I'll say what I have to, then I'll go. Now...in
the first place, you have something against Natasha,
my wife; I've been aware of it since the day we were
married. Natasha is a beautiful and generous person,
direct and honest— that is my opinion. I love and
respect my wife; do you understand? I respect her.

And I demand that others respect her as well. I repeat,
she is an honest and generous person, your
disapproval, excuse me, is simply childish.... *(Pause)*
In the second place, it seems to annoy you that I am
not a professor and not engaged in scholarly study.
But what I am doing now is serving the public. I am
a member of the District Council, and I consider
the work I do to be as worthy, as high-minded, as
anything in a university. I am proud of what I do, if
you want to know.... *(Pause)* In the third place, I have
only one thing more to say.... I mortgaged the house
without asking your permission.... I should not have
done that, and ask to be forgiven.... I had debts to pay
off.... Thirty-five thousand.... I've stopped playing
cards, I stopped a long time ago.... In my own
defense, I can say this, you girls receive Father's
pension, and I get nothing.... In terms of income,
that is.... *(Pause)*

KULYGIN: *(At the door)* Is Masha here? Where is she?
That's odd.... *(Leaves)*

ANDREI: They won't listen. Natasha is a good and
honest person. *(Walks about in silence, then stops)* When
we got married, I thought we'd be happy...all of us....
But oh my God... *(Weeps)* My dear sisters, don't
believe me, don't believe me.... *(He goes)*

(Fire alarm is heard. The stage is empty.)

IRINA: *(From behind her screen)* Olga, who's knocking
on the floor?

OLGA: The Doctor. He's drunk.

IRINA: No rest tonight. *(Pause)* Olga? *(Looks out)*
Did you hear? They're taking the brigade away...
it's going to be transferred somewhere...far away.

OLGA: It's only a rumor.

IRINA: Then we'll be left all alone.... Olga!

OLGA: What?

IRINA: Olga, my dear, I respect the Baron. He's a good person. I do think a lot of him; I'll marry him, I'll say yes, only let's go to Moscow! Please, let's go! Olga, let's go.

END OF ACT THREE

ACT FOUR

(The old garden of the Prozorov house. A long avenue of fir trees, at the end of which can be seen the river. A forest on the other side of the river. On the right of the terrace is the house. Bottles, glasses are on a table right; champagne has recently been drunk. It is mid-day. Every now and then passers-by walk across the garden, from the road to the river; five soldiers go by quickly. CHEBUTYKIN, *in a relaxed frame of mind which he has for the entire act, sits in an armchair in the garden, waiting to be called. He wears a cap and has a stick.* IRINA, KULYGIN, *who now has a cross around his neck and no moustache, and* TUZENBACH *are standing on the terrace seeing* FEDOTIK *and* RODE *off. They are coming down into the garden, both in uniform.)*

TUZENBACH: *(Exchanging hugs with* FEDOTIK*)* You're a good man. We've had some great times together. *(Exchanging hugs with* RODE*)* One more time... Goodbye, my friend.

IRINA: Au revoir!

FEDOTIK: It isn't au revoir, it's goodbye; we won't ever meet again.

KULYGIN: Who knows! *(Wipes his eyes; smiles)*

IRINA: We'll meet again sometime.

FEDOTIK: When? In ten, fifteen years? We'll hardly recognize each other then; we'll ask "How have you been?", but only to be polite.... *(Takes a snapshot)* Don't move.... One more for posterity.

RODE: *(Embracing* TUZENBACH*)* We'll never see each
other again.... *(Kisses* IRINA*'s hand)* Thank you for
everything, for everything!

FEDOTIK: *(Grieved)* Don't move!

TUZENBACH: We'll meet, if it's God's will. Write,
be sure to write.

RODE: *(Looking around the garden)* Goodbye trees!
(Shouts) Yo-ho! *(Pause)* Goodbye echo!

KULYGIN: All the best. Who knows, maybe you'll even
find yourselves a couple of wives in Poland. They'll
embrace you and call you "Kochanku, my
Kochanku!" *(Laughs)*

FEDOTIK: *(Looking at his watch)* Less than an hour left.
Solyony's the only one from our battery going on the
barge; the rest of us are marching. Three batteries
leave today, three more tomorrow, the town will be
calm and quiet then.

TUZENBACH: And very boring.

RODE: Where's Maria Sergheevna?

FEDOTIK: Yes, where's Masha?

KULYGIN: She's in the garden.

FEDOTIK: We'd like to say goodbye to her.

RODE: Goodbye, I better go before I cry.... *(Quickly
embraces* KULYGIN *and* TUZENBACH, *kisses* IRINA*'s
hand)* We've been very happy here.

FEDOTIK: *(To* KULYGIN*)* Here, something to remember
me by...a little notebook with a little pencil... We'll
take the short-cut along the river. *(They go aside and
both look around.)*

RODE: *(Shouts)* Yo-ho!

KULYGIN: *(Shouts)* Goodbye.

(In the background FEDOTIK *and* RODE *meet* MASHA. *They say their goodbyes and leave with her.)*

IRINA: They're gone.... *(Sits on the bottom step of the terrace)*

CHEBUTYKIN: They forgot to say goodbye to me.

IRINA: And what about you?

CHEBUTYKIN: Somehow I forgot too. But I'll see them soon enough. I leave tomorrow...one day left. I'll retire next year and come back to live out my life around you. One more year and I've got my pension. *(Puts a newspaper into his pocket and takes out another)* I'll come back and completely change my life.... I'll become such a quiet, decent, proper little man....

IRINA: Yes, you really do need to change, Ivan Romanych. You must try....

CHEBUTYKIN: Yes, I feel it coming. *(Sings softly)* "Ta ra ra boom de ay, There goes another day."

IRINA: Fyodor's shaved his moustache! I just can't look at him.

KULYGIN: And why not?

CHEBUTYKIN: I could tell you what you now look like, but I'm too polite.

KULYGIN: Well, it is the style now, the modus vivendi. Our principal shaved his off, so when I became his first assistant, I shaved off mine. Nobody likes it, but what do I care. I'm content. With or without a moustache... *(Sits)*

(In the background, ANDREI *is wheeling a baby carriage with a sleeping child.)*

IRINA: I'm very worried, Ivan Romanich. You were in town last night; please, tell me, what happened?

CHEBUTYKIN: What happened? Nothing. Nothing that
matters. *(Reads the paper)* It's all the same.

KULYGIN: What I heard is that Solyony and the Baron
were in front of the theater....

TUZENBACH: Stop it! Really, it's none.... *(Waves his
hand and goes into the house)*

KULYGIN: ...in front of the theater, Solyony started
picking on the Baron, and he blew up, and said
something rather offensive.

CHEBUTYKIN: What do we know? It's just stupid.

KULYGIN: Once a student was struggling with a
question on a test, the teacher walks by, looks at the
paper and says, "That's stupid." So the boy then
wrote in "stupid" for the answer. *(Laughs)* That's very
funny, isn't it? They say Solyony's in love with Irina
and that's why he hates the Baron.... I can understand
that. Irina's a lovely girl. She's like Masha. She's
sensitive.... Though you have a gentler nature, Irina.
Though Masha is very good-natured too. I'm very
fond of her, Masha, I mean. *(Shouts of "Yo-ho!" are
heard off.)*

IRINA: *(Shudders)* I don't know why, but today every
little thing makes me jump. *(Pause)* Everything's
packed, they'll come for my things after lunch.
Tomorrow, the Baron and I will get married;
tomorrow, we'll move close to the brickworks; the
day after I begin teaching school there. When I passed
the teacher's examination, I actually cried, I was so
happy, so thankful.... *(Pause)* The cart will soon be
here for my things....

CHEBUTYKIN: *(With deep feeling)* My dear precious
girl.... Off you go, I can't keep up with you. I've been
left behind; an old migrant bird, too tired to fly. Fly,

dear, fly, and God be with you! *(Pause)* It's a shame
you shaved off your moustache, Fyodor.

KULYGIN: Quit it, will you? *(Sighs)* Today the soldiers
leave and it'll be like the old days again. They can say
what they want, Masha is a good, honest woman. I
love her very much and am grateful for my fate. I've
always been lucky, I'm happy, I've even received the
Saint Stanislaus Cross, second class.... Of course I'm
clever, cleverer than most, but to be happy you need
more than that....

*(The Maiden's Prayer is being played on the piano in the
house.)*

IRINA: One more night and no more listening to this
"Maiden's Prayer," and no more seeing Protopopov.
(Pause) Protopopov's sitting in the living room; he
came even today.

KULYGIN: And the headmistress, isn't she here yet?

IRINA: No. But we've sent for her. If you only knew
how hard it's been to live here alone, without Olga....
She's got her apartment at the school, she's been so
busy being headmistress, and me, I've been alone,
bored, hating the room I live in.... So I made up my
mind if not Moscow, then I guess it's this. It's fate.
If it's God's will, so be it. Nikolai Lvovich asked me
to marry him. And? I thought it over and accepted.
He's a good man.... It's amazing how good he really
is. And suddenly my soul gained wings, I became
happy and light-hearted, and again that craving
for work came over me.... Until yesterday, when
something happened, it's like a mysterious cloud
is hanging over me....

CHEBUTYKIN: That's just silly.

NATASHA: *(At the window:)* The headmistress.

KULYGIN: The headmistress is here. Let's go.

(Leaves with IRINA *into the house)*

CHEBUTYKIN: *(Reads his paper and hums softly)*
"Ta ra ra boom de ay,
There goes another day."

*(*MASHA *approaches.* ANDREI *is wheeling the carriage in the distance.)*

MASHA: Just sitting here, huh....

CHEBUTYKIN: So what?

MASHA: *(Sits)* Nothing... *(Pause)* Did you love my mother?

CHEBUTYKIN: Very much.

MASHA: And did she love you?

CHEBUTYKIN: *(After a pause)* That I no longer remember.

MASHA: Is my man here? That's what our cook, Marta, used to call her sergeant, "my man". Is he here?

CHEBUTYKIN: Not yet.

MASHA: When you've taken your happiness in small bits and then you lose it, as I am losing it now, you begin to grow hard and bitter. *(Points to her breast)* I'm boiling inside.... *(Looks at* ANDREI *and the carriage)* There's our brother Andrei.... All our hopes are gone.... A thousand people were hoisting a bell. Much money and hard work had been spent on making it. But suddenly it fell and broke. Just like that, there was no reason.... The same with Andrei....

ANDREI: Can't they keep it down in there? They're making a lot of noise.

CHEBUTYKIN: It won't be for much longer. *(Looks at his watch)* An old watch, strikes every hour.... *(Winds the watch and makes it strike)* The first, second, and fifth batteries leave at one, on the dot. *(Pause)* I go tomorrow.

ANDREI: For good?

CHEBUTYKIN: I don't know. Maybe I'll come back in a year. Who the hell knows.... It's all the same....

(Somewhere a harp and violin are being played.)

ANDREI: The town will be empty, like someone's put a blanket over it. *(Pause)* Something happened yesterday outside the theater. Everybody's talking about it, only I don't know what went on.

CHEBUTYKIN: Nothing. It's just silly. Solyony annoyed the Baron, who lost his temper and insulted him, so Solyony challenged him to a duel. *(Looks at his watch)* Right around now, I think.... At half past twelve, in the woods, just across the river from here.... Bang-bang! *(Laughs)* Solyony sees himself as Lermontov, he even writes poetry. Fun's fun, but it's already his third duel.

MASHA: Whose?

CHEBUTYKIN: Solyony's.

MASHA: And the Baron?

CHEBUTYKIN: What about the Baron? *(Pause)*

MASHA: I'm confused.... How can such a thing be allowed? He might hurt the Baron, even kill him.

CHEBUTYKIN: A good man, the Baron. But one baron more, one baron less, what's the difference? Let them! It's all the same.

(Beyond the garden somebody shouts)

CHEBUTYKIN: That's Skvortsov, one of the seconds, waiting with the boat.

ANDREI: I think it's immoral to fight a duel, and even to witness one as a doctor; that is my opinion.

CHEBUTYKIN: It seems so, yes.... We also seem to exist, but there's nothing here, we aren't really alive, we only pretend that we are....

MASHA: Talk and talk, day after day.... *(Going)* It's one thing to live in this climate where it can snow at any time, but to have to take all this talk too.... *(Stops)* I won't go into the house, I can't.... *(Goes along the avenue of firs)* The birds have already begun to migrate.... *(Looks up)* Swans or geese...you lovely, happy creatures.... *(Exits)*

ANDREI: The officers are leaving, you are going, my sister is getting married, I'll be left alone in the house.

CHEBUTYKIN: What about your wife?

(FERAPONT enters with some documents.)

ANDREI: A wife is a wife. She's honest, decent, even kind, I grant her all that, still there's something in her that drags her down to the level of a petty, coarse, selfish animal. In any case, she's not human. You're my friend, so I can tell you this, there's no one else I can talk to. I love Natasha, it's true, but there are times when she seems so amazingly vulgar, and I just get confused, I can't understand why I love her, or in any event, once did....

CHEBUTYKIN: *(Getting up)* I leave tomorrow, my friend, and we may never see each other again, so here's my advice. Put on your hat, grab your walking stick, and go...go and don't look back. The farther you go, the better.

(SOLYONY goes across upstage with two officers; he sees CHEBUTYKIN and turns to him. The officers go on.)

SOLYONY: It's time, Doctor. It's already half-past.

(He shakes hands with ANDREI.*)*

CHEBUTYKIN: In a minute. I'm sick and tired of all of you. *(To* ANDREI*)* If they ask, say I'll be back soon.... *(Sighs)* Oh-oh-oh.

SOLYONY: "Before the peasant could even gasp for air, His chest was crushed in the arms of the bear." *(Goes up to him)* What's wrong, old man?

CHEBUTYKIN: What do you care?

SOLYONY: How are you feeling?

CHEBUTYKIN: *(Angrily)* Like a well-oiled machine!

SOLYONY: The old man's gotten all excited over nothing. I won't take him down, just ruffle a feather or two.... I've used a whole bottle of cologne already today...still my hands smell of a corpse. *(Pause)* Yes.... Remember the poem, "And he, the rebel, seeks out the storm, Only there, will he feel safe and warm."?

CHEBUTYKIN: Yes. "Before the peasant could even gasp for air, His chest was crushed in the arms of the bear."

(Leaves with SOLYONY. *Shouts are heard.* ANDREI *and* FERAPONT *come from the back.)*

FERAPONT: Papers to sign.

ANDREI: *(Irritated)* Go away! Leave me alone! *(Goes away with the carriage)*

FERAPONT: That's what papers are for, to be signed.

(Moves to the back of the stage. IRINA *enters with* TUZENBACH, *now in a straw hat;* KULYGIN *walks across the stage, shouting: "Co-ee, Masha, co-ee!")*

TUZENBACH: Here is the only one in town happy to see the soldiers go.

IRINA: You can understand why. *(Pause)* The town will be empty.

TUZENBACH: My dear, I'll be right back.

IRINA: Where are you going?

TUZENBACH: Into town...to say goodbye....

IRINA: That's not true.... All day you've been in a haze, Nikolai. *(Pause)* What happened in front of the theater yesterday?

TUZENBACH: *(With an impatient gesture)* I'll be back, in an hour, I'll be back with you. *(Kisses her hands)* My love.... *(Looking into her face)* Five years ago I fell in love with you, still I'm not used to it, you seem more beautiful every day. Such lovely hair! And eyes! Tomorrow I'll take you away. We'll work, we'll make our fortune, my dreams will come true. You will be happy. There's just one small thing, you don't love me.

IRINA: That's not in my power. I will be your wife, I'll be faithful and obedient, everything, but love you. I can't make myself. *(Cries)* I've never been in love in my life.... I've begun to think of my heart as one of those expensive pianos that's been locked, the key lost. *(Pause)* You seem restless.

TUZENBACH: I couldn't sleep last night. The only fear I have in the world is that I won't find that lost key. This keeps me from sleeping. Say something. *(Pause)* Say something to me.

IRINA: What? What do you want me to say? What?

TUZENBACH: Something.

IRINA: No! No!*(Pause)*

TUZENBACH: Funny, isn't it, how the stupidest thing, for no real reason, can suddenly become so important. First you try to laugh it off, you think what the hell, but soon you find you haven't the strength to put a stop to it. But let's not talk about that. I am happy. I think for the first time in my life, I'm really seeing these elms, maples, birches; they all seem to be watching me, and waiting. They are beautiful, and when you think about it, life in a world which has such trees can't be anything but beautiful! *(Shouts in the distance)* I better go. It's time.... Look, that tree is dead, but it still sways in the breeze with the others. Maybe it'll be the same for me if I die, I'll still be a part of life, in one form or another. Good-bye, dear.... *(Kisses her hand)* The papers you gave me are on my table, under the calendar.

IRINA: I'm coming with you.

TUZENBACH: *(Nervously)* No, no! *(He goes quickly and stops.)* Irina!

IRINA: What?

TUZENBACH: *(He doesn't know what to say.)* I haven't had any coffee today. Please tell them to make me some....

(He goes out quickly. IRINA stands, deep in thought. Then she goes upstage and sits in a swing. ANDREI comes in with the carriage; FERAPONT also appears.)

FERAPONT: Andrei Sergheevich, it isn't like these papers were mine, they're the government's. I didn't pull them out of a hat.

ANDREI: Dear God, what's happened to me? Where'd my life go? I used to be young, happy, thoughtful. I had ideas, dreams, I had a future. Why is it, that before we even begin to live, we're already dulled, gray, lazy, boring, useless, unhappy?... This town is two hundred years old, it has one hundred thousand people. In all that time, out of all those people, not one man who thinks his own thoughts, not one

scholar, artist, no one important enough to envy or
admire. They only eat, drink, sleep, die.... And more
are born who eat, drink, sleep; and to keep the
boredom from driving them completely crazy,
they expand their great intellects with vodka, cards,
litigations, and back-biting gossip. Wives cheat on
husbands, husbands lie and say they see nothing,
hear nothing. Such evil infects the children,
extinguishing in them God's glow, until they become
but pitiful corpses indistinguishable from each other,
as are their fathers and mothers.... *(Angrily to*
FERAPONT*)* What is it now?

FERAPONT: What? Papers to be signed.

ANDREI: I'm so sick of you.

FERAPONT: *(Handing him the papers)* The porter at the
courthouse just told me that in the winter it was two
hundred degrees below zero in St. Petersburg.

ANDREI: The present is disgusting, but there's the
future and it will be good! Just thinking about it
calms me, frees me; there is a light in the dark, I see
freedom, for myself and my children, freedom from
life's vanities, its vodka, its goose and cabbage, its
afternoon naps, its wasted lives....

FERAPONT: He said two thousand people froze to
death. This was in St. Petersburg, or Moscow, I forget
which one.

ANDREI: *(Overcome with tender emotion)* My dear
sisters, my wonderful sisters! *(Crying)* Masha, my
sister....

NATASHA: *(At the window)* Who's yelling out there?
Is that you, Andrei? You'll wake up Sofichka! Il ne
faut pas faire du bruit, la Sophie est dormée déja.
Vous etes un ours. *(Angrily)* If you want to yell, give
someone else the carriage. Ferapont, take the carriage!

FERAPONT: Yes, Ma'am. *(Takes the carriage)*

ANDREI: *(Intimidated)* I'll talk quieter.

NATASHA: *(At the window, to Bobik)* Bobik! Stop it! Bad boy!

ANDREI: *(Looking through the papers)* All right, I'll look these over and sign where I'm supposed to and you can take them back to the office.... *(Goes into the house, reading the papers)*

(FERAPONT pushes the carriage to the back of the garden.)

NATASHA: *(At the window)* Now Bobik, who is mommy? Good boy! And who is that lady there? That is your Aunt Olga. Say, "Hello, Aunt Olga!"

(VERSHININ, OLGA, and ANFISA come out of the house. IRINA walks up to them.)

ANFISA: *(To IRINA)* My Irina! *(Kisses her)* My little girl, here I am, still alive! Still alive! I'm at the high school with Olga in her official government apartment.... So the Good Lord protected me after all. A sinful old woman's never had it so good.... The apartment's huge, it's official government property; I have a whole room just for me and a bed, too, everything official government property. I wake up at night and think, dear Mother of God, I am the happiest person alive!

VERSHININ: *(Looks at his watch)* They'll be leaving soon, Olga, I should go. *(Pause)* I wish you all the happiness in the world—all the happiness.... Have you seen Masha?

IRINA: She's in the garden, I'll go and get her.

VERSHININ: If you would, I haven't much time.

ANFISA: I'll go and get her, too. *(Shouts)* Masha, little Masha, yoo-hoo! *(Goes out with IRINA down into the garden)* Yoo-hoo! Yoo-hoo!

VERSHININ: Everything comes to an end. And so, we must part. *(Looks at his watch)* The town gave us a kind of goodbye breakfast—champagne, a speech by the mayor. I ate, I listened, but my heart was here.... *(Looks around the garden)* I've grown so used to all of you.

OLGA: Will we ever see each other again?

VERSHININ: Most likely not. *(Pause)* My wife and daughters are staying another two months. If something happens, if they need anything....

OLGA: Yes, of course. Yes. Don't you worry. *(Pause)* Tomorrow, not a soldier will be left in town, it will all be a memory; and for us a new life begins.... *(Pause)* Nothing's worked out as we hoped. I never wanted to be headmistress, but I am. Now there's no hope of going to Moscow....

VERSHININ: My, my...thank you for everything. I'm sorry if I have...if I have done.... And if at times I've talked too much, I'm sorry for that too. Don't think badly of me.

OLGA: *(Wipes her eyes)* Why isn't Masha coming?...

VERSHININ: What's left to say? We could talk philosophy.... *(Laughs)* Life is hard. To so many of us it seems just bleak and hopeless; but we have to keep remembering that it is getting brighter and better; and in not too many years, it will even be good. *(Looks at his watch)* I have to go! The world once spent its energies on war, life was a series of campaigns, battles, defeats. Having outgrown all that now, we've been left with a hole because we have not found anything to replace it with. But we are looking and it will be found. I just wish it wouldn't take so long. *(Pause)* If we could only bring what we know together with what we do, bring together what we do with what we know.... *(Looks at his watch)* I have to go....

OLGA: Here she comes.

(MASHA *enters.*)

VERSHININ: I came to say good-bye.

(OLGA *steps aside a little, so as not to be in their way.*)

MASHA: (*Looking him in the face*) Good-bye...
(*She gives him a lingering kiss.*)

OLGA: Don't! Don't! (MASHA *breaks into tears.*)

VERSHININ: Write to me... Don't forget. Let me go...it's
time. Take her, Olga.... It's time.... I'm late.
(*He kisses* OLGA's *hand in evident emotion, then embraces*
MASHA *once more and goes out quietly.*)

OLGA: Please, Masha! Don't, dear!...

(KULYGIN *enters.*)

KULYGIN: (*Uneasy*) Let her. Let her cry. Let her....
My dear Masha, my good Masha... You're my wife,
and I'm content, for better or worse.... I'm not
complaining, I am not accusing you...Olga's my
witness.... We'll start living again, as we used to....
I won't ever say a word, or give you the slightest
look....

MASHA: (*Holding back her sobs*) "A green oak stands
by the sea, A golden chain around it... A golden chain
around it..." I'm going crazy.... "A green oak
stands...by the sea.... A golden chain..."

OLGA: Calm down, Masha, calm down...give her
some water...

MASHA: I'm not crying anymore.

KULYGIN: She's not crying anymore.... She's a good....
(*A shot is heard in the distance*)

MASHA: "A green oak stands by the sea, A golden
chain around it..." A green cat...green oak.... I'm

getting mixed up.... *(Drinks some water)* Life is bleak....
There's nothing left that I want.... I'll be fine in a
minute.... It's nothing.... What do those lines mean?
Why can't I get them out of my head? It's all like a
knot.

(IRINA enters.)

OLGA: Calm down, Masha. There, there... Let's go in.

MASHA: *(Angrily)* I'm not going in there. *(Sobs, but
immediately controls herself)* I'm not going into that
house, I'm not....

IRINA: Then let's sit here, we don't have to talk. I leave
tomorrow.... *(Pause)*

KULYGIN: I found this beard in the desk of one of my
students yesterday.... *(Puts on the beard)* Don't I look
like our German teacher?... *(Laughs)* I do, don't I? The
boys are so funny.

MASHA: You do look like the German teacher.

OLGA: *(Laughs)* You do.

(MASHA weeps.)

IRINA: Don't, Masha.

KULYGIN: I could be his double.

(NATASHA enters.)

NATASHA: *(To the maid)* What? Protopopov can keep
an eye on Sofichka, and Andrei can take Bobik for
a walk. Children, they never give you a moment's
peace.... *(To IRINA)* Irina, it's a pity you have to leave
tomorrow, do stay... for another week.

*(She sees KULYGIN and screams; he laughs and takes off his
beard.)*

NATASHA: You scared me! *(To IRINA)* I've gotten so
used to having you around, it won't be easy to give

you up. I'm putting Andrei and his violin in your room, fiddle up there all he wants, Sofichka can have his room. What a beautiful, lovely girl! Today she looked up at me with those pretty little eyes and said: "Mommy!"

KULYGIN: A beautiful child, it's quite true.

NATASHA: So, tomorrow I'll be here all alone. *(Sighs)* First off, those trees have to be cut down. And then those maples. They're so ugly and scary at night.... *(To* IRINA*)* That belt, dear, just doesn't suit you.... What's happened to your taste? You must wear something brighter. I'll give orders that I want lots and lots of flowers planted here, that'll smell nice and maybe a fountain painted pink.... What's this fork doing on this chair? *(Going toward the house, to the maid)* What was this fork doing on that chair? *(Shouts)* Don't you dare talk back to me! *(Goes)*

KULYGIN: There she goes....

(A march is played off; they all listen.)

OLGA: They're leaving.

*(*CHEBUTYKIN *comes in.)*

MASHA: They're leaving.... My, my... Bon voyage. *(To her husband)* We should go home.... Where's my hat and coat?

KULYGIN: In the house. I'll get them in a minute.

OLGA: Yes, we can all go home now. It's time.

CHEBUTYKIN: Olga!

OLGA: What is it? *(Pause)* What is it?

CHEBUTYKIN: Nothing really.... How shall I put it?... *(Whispers to her)*

OLGA: *(Frightened)* I don't believe it!

CHEBUTYKIN: Yes...that's the story...I'm tired, empty, I've said enough.... *(Sadly)* And it's all the same.

MASHA: What's happened?

OLGA: *(Embraces* IRINA*)* It's terrible.... I don't know if I can tell you.... My dear!

IRINA: What is it? Quick, tell me, what it is? For God's sake! *(Cries)*

CHEBUTYKIN: The Baron has been killed in the duel.

IRINA: *(Cries softly)* I knew it, I knew it....

CHEBUTYKIN: *(Sits on a bench upstage)* I'm tired.... *(Takes a paper from his pocket)* Let them cry.... *(Sings softly)* "Ta ra ra boom de ay, There goes another day." Really, it's all the same.

(The three sisters are standing, pressing against one another.)

MASHA: Listen—the music! They're leaving us, everyone has left forever and ever, we're left alone to start again. We must keep living.... We must keep living....

IRINA: *(Puts her head on* OLGA*'s breast)* The time will come when everyone will know the reason for this suffering and there will be no more mysteries. We must keep living...we must work, just work! Tomorrow I'll go away alone, I'll teach and devote the rest of my life to others who may need it. It's fall now, then winter, and the snow will cover over everything, and I shall work, just work....

OLGA: *(Embraces both her sisters)* The way the band is playing, it sounds so happy, so brave, you do want to keep living. My God, time will go by and we will be dead forever; they will forget our faces, voices, even how many we were, but upon our suffering, their joy will be built, happiness and peace will rule the world, and we who live today will be spoken kindly of and thanked. Dear sisters, our lives aren't over yet. Let us live. The music is happy and alive, and it seems that some time soon we will know why we live, why we suffer.... If only we knew. If only we knew.

(The music has been growing softer and softer; KULYGIN, smiling happily, brings out the hat and coat; ANDREI wheels out the carriage.)

CHEBUTYKIN: *(Sings softly)* "Ta ra ra boom de ay, There goes another day." *(Reads a paper)* It's all the same! It's all the same!

OLGA: If only we knew! If only we knew!

END OF PLAY